Good Housekeeping
Cookery Club

Cakes & Biscuits

Joanna Farrow

EBURY PRESS
LONDON

First published 1994

1 3 5 7 9 10 8 6 4 2

Text and Photography © Ebury Press 1994

First published in the United Kingdom in 1994 by Ebury Press
Random House, 20 Vauxhall Bridge Road, London SW1V 2SA

Random House Australia (Pty) Limited
20 Alfred Street, Milsons Point, Sydney,
New South Wales 2061, Australia

Random House New Zealand Limited
18 Poland Road, Glenfield,
Auckland 10, New Zealand

Random House South Africa (Pty) Limited
PO Box 337, Bergvlei, South Africa

Random House UK Limited Reg. No. 954009

A CIP catalogue record for this book is available from the British Library.

Managing Editor: JANET ILLSLEY
Design: SARA KIDD
Special Photography: GRAHAM KIRK
Food Stylist: JOANNA FARROW
Photographic Stylist: HELEN PAYNE
Techniques Photography: KARL ADAMSON
Recipe Testing: EMMA-LEE GOW

ISBN 0 09 179 000 X

Typeset in Gill Sans by Textype Typesetters, Cambridge
Colour Separations by Magnacraft, London
Printed and bound in Italy by New Interlitho Italia S.p.a., Milan

CONTENTS

COOKERY NOTES

- Both metric and imperial measures are given for the recipes. Follow either metric or imperial throughout as they are not interchangeable.
- All spoon measures are level unless otherwise stated. Sets of measuring spoons are available in both metric and imperial sizes for accurate measurement of small quantities.
- Ovens should be preheated to the specified temperature. Grills should also be preheated. The cooking times given in the recipes assume that this has been done.
- If a stage is specified under freezing instructions, the dish should be frozen at the end of that stage.
- Size 2 eggs should be used except where otherwise specified. Free-range eggs are recommended.

INTRODUCTION

There is nothing quite like the warm, enticing aroma of a freshly baked cake, teabread or tray of biscuits to give us a nostalgic boost. At other times, it may be a richly indulgent gâteau or a smart celebration centrepiece that is called for. In this varied collection, you will find recipes to suit all kinds of occasions.

Many of the recipes are quick and easy – perfect for impromptu baking – and for inexperienced bakers, there is a useful step-by-step guide to basic techniques.

BASIC INGREDIENTS

As with any type of cooking, the use of good basic ingredients is important. Unsalted butter, rich and creamy in flavour, gives best results in most recipes. Those who are more health-conscious may prefer to substitute margarine, but low-fat 'spreads' should be avoided as they are high in water and have a synthetic flavour. Most cake recipes require the fat to be used at room temperature. If necessary you can soften it, cautiously, in the microwave.

Eggs should also be used at room temperature; if taken straight from the refrigerator they are more likely to curdle a cake mixture. Make sure you use the correct size too – unless otherwise stated 'size 2' eggs should be used in all of these recipes.

Self-raising white flour is used in most cake recipes as it has added raising agent, whereas plain white flour is generally used for biscuits and cookies. Plain or self-raising wholemeal flour can be substituted although the results will be darker, denser and nuttier in flavour. Half white and half wholemeal makes a good compromise if you want to incorporate extra fibre. If you sieve it before use don't forget to tip the bran left in the sieve into the bowl.

Caster sugar is generally used for cakes, but light or dark muscovado sugars can be substituted for a richer colour and flavour.

Other storecupboard ingredients such as nuts, dried fruits and spices are frequently included in cakes and biscuits. Although good 'keepers' they shouldn't be bought in bulk as they do eventually stale. Keep an eye on the use-by dates.

EQUIPMENT

Little is needed in the way of cake-making equipment for these recipes, other than scales, basic bowls, spoons, etc. A hand-held electric whisk takes all the effort out of creaming and whisking, while a food processor is perfect for cakes that involve rubbing the fat into the flour.

Good quality cake tins are essential, and it is important to use the tin size stated in the recipe. For storage convenience, adjustable square tins are now available, in which the sides can be reduced or enlarged as required. Quality baking sheets are a worthwhile investment too. Choose ones that are large (but fit comfortably into your oven) to avoid baking in several batches.

When baking cakes, avoid the temptation of looking in the oven well before the end of the cooking time as the sudden gust of cool air might make the cake sink. Instead wait until the cooking time is almost up before testing. Apart from very light sponges, all cakes are best left to stand in their tin for several minutes after baking to firm up slightly. Biscuits, with their high sugar content, will seem very soft after baking. These too, should be left on the baking sheet before transferring to a wire rack.

STORAGE

Some of the cake and biscuit recipes specify storage times. With the exception of rich fruit cakes and gingerbread, most cakes and biscuits are best enjoyed freshly baked. If storing is necessary, use a cake tin or large plastic container. Failing this, wrap in greaseproof paper, then foil.

Most cakes, particularly sponges, freeze beautifully, but preferably before they're filled and decorated. If freezing a finished gâteau, open freeze, and then pack in a rigid container. Biscuits should never be stored in the same tin as a cake, and preferably not with other types of biscuits, as they quickly soften and absorb other flavours.

PREPARATION TECHNIQUES

Successful baking is at least partly dependant on the use of good basic techniques, such as lining and filling tins, whisking, folding in, etc. The following step-by-step guides apply to many of the recipes.

PREPARING TINS

With most cakes it is necessary to line the tins with greaseproof paper, or non-stick baking parchment. The latter is used for cakes which are more likely to stick, such as roulades and meringues.

LINING A SQUARE TIN

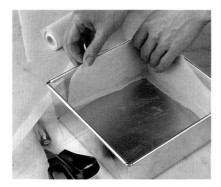

Cut a square of greaseproof paper fractionally smaller than the base of the tin. For the sides, cut strips about 2 cm (¾ inch) wider than the depth of the tin. Fold up the bottom edge by I cm (½ inch). Grease the tin. Make a cut from the edge of the paper to the fold and press into one corner. Continue fitting the paper around the tin, cutting to fit at each corner. Lay the square of paper in the base, then grease all the paper.

LINING A ROUND TIN

Place the tin on a piece of greaseproof paper and draw around it. Cut out, just inside the line. Cut strip(s) of paper, about 2 cm (¾ inch) wider than the depth of the tin. Fold up bottom edge by I cm (½ inch), then make cuts, 2.5 cm (I inch) apart, from edge to fold. Grease tin. Position paper strip(s) around side of tin so snipped edge sits on base. Lay paper circle in base, then grease all the paper.

LINING A LOAF TIN

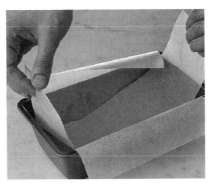

Grease base and sides of loaf tin. Cut

a strip of greaseproof paper, the length of the tin base and wide enough to cover the base and long sides. Press into position. Cut another strip, the width of the tin base and long enough to cover the base and ends of the tin. Press into position. Grease all the paper.

NOTE: Sometimes only the base and long sides of a loaf tin need lining. In this case, use a double thickness of paper so that the cake can easily be lifted from tin (see Cherry Streusel Slice – page 56).

LINING A SWISS ROLL TIN OR SHALLOW BAKING TIN

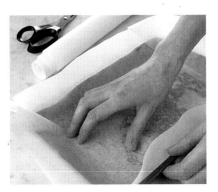

Grease base and sides of tin. Cut a rectangle of greaseproof or non-stick baking parchment, 7.5 cm (3 inches) wider and longer than the size of the tin. Press the paper into the tin, cutting the paper at the corners and folding to fit neatly. Grease the paper.

PREPARING SANDWICH TINS

Place sandwich tin on a piece of greaseproof paper and draw around it. Cut out, just inside the line. Grease base and sides of tin and fit paper into base. Grease paper. Sprinkle a little flour into tin. Tap and tilt the tin until flour coats the base and sides. Tip out excess flour.

WRAPPING FOR FRUIT CAKES

To prevent the edges of a fruit cake overcooking, wrap the tin in brown paper. First line the inside, then cut a double thick strip of brown paper, the circumference of the tin and 2.5 cm (1 inch) deeper. Position around the tin, securing with string.

CAKE-MAKING TECHNIQUES

CREAMING METHOD

1. Beat together the softened butter or margarine and sugar until pale and fluffy and very light in consistency. Use an electric whisk, or a wooden spoon – which will require longer vigorous beating. Scrape the mixture down from the sides of the bowl frequently to ensure an evenly creamed mixture.

2. Using a wooden spoon or electric whisk, beat in the eggs, a little at a time, beating well after each addition. Use eggs at room temperature and beat thoroughly after each addition to ensure the mixture does not curdle. If it curdles a heavier cake will result. To prevent curdling, a little of the measured flour can be added with the eggs.

3. Sift the flour over the creamed mixture, sifting high so that plenty of air is incorporated. Use a larger metal spoon to gently fold in the flour, cutting and folding into the mixture using a figure-of-eight movement.

NOTE: When mixing an 'all-in-one' cake, the ingredients are beaten to a similarly creamy consistency in one go. Ensure that the butter or margarine is completely softened before mixing with the remaining ingredients. If the mixture seems firm once creamed, beat in a dash of milk so that it drops easily from the spoon when gently tapped against the side of the bowl.

WHISKING METHOD

1. Put the eggs and sugar in a large heatproof bowl over a pan of hot water and whisk until the mixture is thick enough to leave a trail when the whisk is lifted from the bowl. Remove the bowl from the heat and continue whisking for about 5 minutes or until cool.

2. Sift half the flour over the mixture. Using a large metal spoon, gently cut and fold the flour into the whisked mixture. Sift remaining flour onto mixture and lightly fold in, until only just incorporated. Do not over-mix or the sponge mixture will reduce in volume.

GENOESE SPONGE

This is made by the whisking method, but melted butter is added with the flour. The butter must be cool and beginning to thicken otherwise it will be difficult to incorporate.

1. Once half the flour has been folded into the whisked mixture (see left), gradually pour the cooled butter around the edge of the bowl.

2. Sift remaining flour over bowl and gently cut and fold it in as lightly as possible.

BAKING CAKES

TURNING CAKE MIXTURE INTO TIN

Spoon the cake mixture into the tin, dividing it evenly between the tins if making a sandwich cake. Use a palette knife to spread the cake mixture in an even layer, right to the edges.

TURNING WHISKED SPONGE MIXTURE INTO TIN

Pour the whisked mixture into the tin and tilt the tin so that the mixture spreads to the edges. If necessary use a plastic spatula to *gently* spread the mixture into the corners. Avoid over-spreading as this will crush the air bubbles.

TESTING SPONGES AFTER BAKING

Carefully remove cake from oven and touch the centre with one hand. It should feel spongy and give very slightly. With whisked cakes the sponge should just be shrinking from the sides of the tin. If necessary return the cake to the oven for a few minutes, closing the door very gently so that vibration does not cause the cake to sink in the centre.

TESTING FRUIT CAKES AFTER BAKING

Remove cake from oven, insert a skewer into the centre and remove. The skewer should come away cleanly. If any cake mixture is sticking to the skewer, return cake to oven for a little longer.

TURNING OUT CAKES

Sponge cakes should be removed from the tin immediately after baking. First loosen the edges and then invert onto a wire cooling rack. If preferred, place a sheet of non-stick baking parchment dusted with sugar over the rack before inverting, so that the soft sponge does not stick to the rack.

NOTE: Semi-rich fruit cakes should be left to cool in the tin for about 15 minutes, while rich fruit cakes are left to cool completely in the tin as they tend to break up if removed while still warm.

COVERING A CAKE WITH ALMOND PASTE

1. Trim top of cake level. Turn cake over so flat bottom becomes top.

2. Roll out half the almond paste on a surface dusted with icing sugar to fit top of cake. Brush cake top with apricot glaze.

3. Lift almond paste onto cake and smooth over, neatening the edges. Place on a cake board, which should be at least 5 cm (2 inches) larger than the cake.

4. Cut a piece of string the same height as the cake with its almond paste top, and another to fit around the side of the cake. Roll out the remaining almond paste and, using the string as a guide, trim the paste to size. Brush the sides of the cake and the almond paste rim with apricot glaze.

5. Roll up the almond paste strip loosely. Place one end against the side of the cake and unroll to cover the sides of the cake. Use a palette knife to smooth over the sides and joins of the paste.

6. Flatten the top lightly with a rolling pin. Leave the cake in a cool, dry room to dry out thoroughly for about 2 days before applying the icing.

APPLYING SUGARPASTE

1. Dust the work surface and rolling pin with cornflour. Knead the icing until pliable. Roll out into a round or square 5-7.5 cm (2-3 inches) larger than the cake all round.

2. With the help of a rolling pin, lift the icing on top of the cake and allow it to drape over the edges. Dust your hands with cornflour and press the icing onto the sides of the cake, easing it down to the board.

3. Trim off excess icing at base.

4. Using your fingers dusted with a little cornflour, gently rub the surface in a circular movement to buff the icing and make it smooth.

ESPRESSO CAKES

Richly flavoured, yet delicately proportioned, these small cakes make an interesting variation on a regular coffee sponge. A creamy custard, flavoured with chopped chocolate-coated coffee beans and ground espresso is sandwiched between light-as-air circles of whisked sponge. Both sponge and filling can be made a day in advance and assembled shortly before serving.

MAKES 7

3 eggs
75 g (3 oz) light or dark
    muscovado sugar
75 g (3 oz) plain white flour
MOCHA CUSTARD
15 g (½ oz) chocolate-coated
    coffee beans
40 g (1½ oz) caster sugar
20 g (¾ oz) cornflour
2 egg yolks
2.5 ml (½ tsp) vanilla essence
200 ml (7 fl oz) milk
90 ml (3 fl oz) double cream
30 ml (2 tbsp) finely ground
    espresso coffee
TO ASSEMBLE
cocoa powder, for dusting
90 ml (3 fl oz) double cream
10 ml (2 tsp) finely ground
    espresso coffee
chopped chocolate-coated
    coffee beans, to decorate

PREPARATION TIME
30 minutes, plus cooling
COOKING TIME
10-12 minutes
FREEZING
Suitable: Sponge only

280 CALS PER CAKE

1. Preheat the oven to 200°C (400°F) Mark 6. Grease and line a 33 × 23 cm (13 × 9 inch) Swiss roll tin.

2. Put the eggs and sugar in a large heat-proof bowl over a pan of simmering water and whisk until the mixture is thick enough to leave a trail on the surface when the whisk is lifted. Remove bowl from pan and whisk until cooled.

3. Sift the flour over the whisked mixture and fold in carefully, using a large metal spoon. Turn into the prepared tin, gently easing the mixture into the corners. Bake for 10-12 minutes until well risen and just firm. Turn out onto a clean sheet of greaseproof paper and peel away the lining paper.

4. To make the custard, finely chop the chocolate-coated coffee beans. Place the sugar, cornflour, egg yolks, vanilla essence and a little of the milk in a bowl and beat until smooth. Put the rest of the milk, the cream and coffee in a saucepan and bring to the boil. Pour over the custard, stirring until smooth. Return to the heat and cook, stirring, for 2-3 minutes until thickened. Transfer to a bowl and cover the surface with a piece of greaseproof paper to prevent a skin forming. Leave to cool.

5. Using a 6 cm (2½ inch) metal cutter, cut out 14 rounds from the sponge.

6. Spoon a little custard onto half of the rounds, then top with the remaining sponges. Dust generously with cocoa powder. Whip the cream until just peaking and spoon a little on top of each cake. Sprinkle with the ground espresso and decorate each cake with chopped chocolate-coated coffee beans. Chill until ready to serve.

NOTE: Espresso coffee gives a strong flavour. Use a milder coffee if preferred.

TECHNIQUE

Spoon a little of the custard onto half of the sponge rounds, spreading it almost to the edges. Gently press the remaining sponges on top.

HONEY AND YOGURT MUFFINS

American style muffins rise considerably during baking to produce a wonderful craggy texture and typically 'top heavy' appearance. This honey and yogurt version is light, airy and perfect served with just a dot of butter while still warm. For a sweeter variation, try the rippled chocolate and banana variation.

MAKES 12

225 g (8 oz) plain white flour

7.5 ml (1½ tsp) baking powder

5 ml (1 tsp) bicarbonate of soda

pinch of salt

2.5 ml (½ tsp) ground mixed spice

1.25 ml (¼ tsp) ground nutmeg

50 g (2 oz) medium oatmeal

50 g (2 oz) light muscovado sugar

50 g (2 oz) butter

225 g (8 oz) Greek-style yogurt

125 ml (4 fl oz) milk

1 egg

60 ml (4 tbsp) clear honey

medium oatmeal, for dusting

PREPARATION TIME
15 minutes
COOKING TIME
17-20 minutes
FREEZING
Suitable

180 CALS PER MUFFIN

1. Preheat the oven to 200°C (400°F) Mark 6. Line 12 deep bun tins or muffin tins with paper muffin cases. Sift the flour, baking powder, bicarbonate of soda, salt, mixed spice and nutmeg into a bowl. Stir in the oatmeal and sugar.

2. Melt the butter and leave to cool slightly. Mix the yogurt and milk together in a bowl, then beat in the egg, butter and honey.

3. Pour over the dry ingredients and stir in quickly until only just blended; do not over-mix.

4. Divide the mixture equally between the paper cases. Sprinkle with oatmeal and bake for 17-20 minutes until well risen and just firm to the touch. Remove from the oven and leave in the tins for 5 minutes, then transfer to a wire rack. Serve warm or cold, with a little butter if desired.

CHOCOLATE BANANA MUFFINS

Omit the honey. Mash 1 small ripe banana and mix with 125 g (4 oz) melted plain chocolate. Add to the muffin mixture after the liquids, blending until rippled with colour.

TECHNIQUE

Quickly stir the liquid into the dry ingredients. Do not over-mix – the dough should be lumpy with specks of flour still visible.

HINNY CAKES WITH SUGARED BLUEBERRIES

These moist teatime cakes, spiced with mace and cloves, are pan-fried to give a soft, spongy texture on the inside and a sweet, crisp crust. Once fried, they're topped with fresh blueberries and caster sugar, then lightly grilled to bring out the full scented flavour of the berries.

MAKES 10

175 g (6 oz) self-raising
   white flour
pinch of salt
5 ml (1 tsp) baking powder
1.25 ml (¼ tsp) ground mace
1.25 ml (¼ tsp) ground
   cloves
75 g (3 oz) unsalted butter
25 g (1 oz) ground rice
25 g (1 oz) caster sugar
90 ml (3 fl oz) milk
30 ml (2 tbsp) sunflower oil
TO FINISH
225-350 g (8-12 oz)
   blueberries
40 g (1½ oz) caster sugar
lightly whipped cream, to
   serve

PREPARATION TIME
10 minutes
COOKING TIME
14-18 minutes
FREEZING
Not suitable

190 CALS PER CAKE

1. Sift the flour, salt, baking powder, mace and cloves into a bowl. Add 50 g (2 oz) of the butter, cut into small pieces, and rub in using the fingertips until the mixture resembles fine breadcrumbs. Stir in the ground rice and caster sugar. Add the milk and mix to a fairly soft dough, using a round-bladed knife.

2. Turn the dough out onto a lightly floured surface and knead very lightly. Cut into 10 even-sized pieces. Using lightly floured hands, shape each piece into a small flat cake.

3. Melt 15 g (½ oz) of the remaining butter with half the oil in a large heavy-based frying pan or griddle. Place half of the cakes in the pan and fry gently for 3-4 minutes until golden underneath. Turn the cakes over and cook for a further 3-4 minutes until cooked through. Transfer to a large baking sheet. Melt the remaining butter with the oil and fry the rest of the cakes.

4. Preheat the grill to medium. Spoon the blueberries onto the cakes, piling them up slightly in the centre. Sprinkle with the sugar. Place under the grill for about 2 minutes, watching closely, until the blueberries are bubbling and the cake edges are lightly toasted. Serve immediately, with whipped cream.

NOTE: It is essential to cook the cakes over a very gentle heat. A high temperature will overcook the crusts while the centres remain raw.

VARIATIONS

Use cranberries, or a mixture of dessert apples and blackberries instead of the blueberries. Serve with mascarpone cheese or Greek-style yogurt rather than whipped cream.

TECHNIQUE

Shape the dough into a log, then cut into 10 even-sized pieces. Using lightly floured hands, shape each piece into a flat cake.

CITRUS ECCLES CAKES

Flaky, light and oozing butter, these delicate lattice-topped pastries are a far cry from some dry and heavy shop-bought versions. In this recipe they are filled with currants, citrus peel and muscovado sugar, and drizzled with melted butter after cooking. For maximum enjoyment serve with that freshly baked lingering warmth.

MAKES 20

PASTRY
175 g (6 oz) firm unsalted
   butter
225 g (8 oz) plain white flour
pinch of salt
5 ml (1 tsp) lemon juice
FILLING
175 g (6 oz) currants
50 g (2 oz) chopped mixed
   peel
50 g (2 oz) muscovado sugar
finely grated rind of
   2 lemons
TO FINISH
beaten egg, to glaze
caster sugar, for dusting
50 g (2 oz) unsalted butter

PREPARATION TIME
35 minutes, plus chilling
COOKING TIME
12-15 minutes
FREEZING
Suitable

160 CALS PER CAKE

1. To make the pastry, cut the butter into small dice. Sift the flour and salt into a bowl. Add the butter, lemon juice and 100 ml (3½ fl oz) iced water. Using a round-bladed knife mix to a soft dough, adding a little extra water if it is too dry.

2. Knead lightly, then roll out on a lightly floured surface to an oblong, about 30 cm (12 inches) long and 10 cm (4 inches) wide. Fold the bottom third up and the lower third down, keeping the edges straight, then give the pastry a quarter turn. Repeat the rolling, folding and turning four more times. Wrap in greaseproof paper and leave to rest in the refrigerator for 30 minutes.

3. For the filling, mix the currants, mixed peel, sugar and lemon rind together in a small bowl.

4. Preheat the oven to 220°C (425°F) Mark 7. Lightly grease two baking sheets. Roll out half of the pastry on a lightly floured surface to a 50×20 cm (20×8 inch) rectangle. Cut in half lengthways, then cut each strip into five equal pieces.

5. Using the tip of a knife make three 2 cm (¾ inch) cuts, 5 mm (¼ inch) apart down the centre of one piece of pastry. Make three more rows of cuts either side of the first row so that when the pastry is pulled apart slightly it creates a lattice. Repeat with remaining pieces of pastry. Brush edges with beaten egg.

6. Set aside half of the filling. Divide the remainder between the latticed pastries, placing it in the centres. Bring the edges of the pastry up over the filling, pinching them together to seal. Invert onto one baking sheet, so the latticed sides face upwards.

7. Repeat with the remaining pastry and filling to make ten more pastries. Brush the pastries with beaten egg and sprinkle lightly with sugar. Bake for 12-15 minutes, until golden. Melt the butter and pour a little into each Eccles cake, through the lattice. Serve warm.

CHERRY AND ALMOND CAKES

Replace currants, peel and lemon rind with 125 g (4 oz) chopped glacé cherries, 50 g (2 oz) chopped blanched almonds and 125 g (4 oz) grated almond paste.

TECHNIQUE

Make rows of cuts in the pastry 5 mm (¼ inch) apart and stagger the rows to shape the lattice.

SAFFRON SCONES

With its golden colour, wonderful aroma and intriguing taste, regal saffron gives an exciting lift to the humble scone. Serve warm with melting butter or generous scoops of thick clotted cream. Slices of juicy melon and mango would make the perfect accompaniment.

MAKES ABOUT 12

½-1 sachet or 2.5-5 ml
(½-1 tsp) saffron strands
(see note)
150 ml (¼ pint) milk
(approximately)
225 g (8 oz) self-raising
white flour
pinch of salt
5 ml (1 tsp) baking powder
40 g (1½ oz) firm unsalted
butter or margarine
30 ml (2 tbsp) caster sugar
beaten egg, to glaze

PREPARATION TIME
15 minutes, plus infusing
COOKING TIME
10-12 minutes
FREEZING
Suitable

110 CALS PER SCONE

1. Preheat the oven to 220°C (425°F) Mark 7. Lightly grease a baking sheet. Roughly break up the saffron strands and place in a saucepan with half of the milk. Bring just to the boil, then remove from the heat and leave to infuse for 20 minutes.

2. Sift the flour, salt and baking powder into a bowl. Add the butter, cut into small pieces, and rub in using the fingertips until the mixture resembles fine breadcrumbs. Stir in the sugar.

3. Stir in the saffron milk and half of the remaining milk. Mix with a round-bladed knife to a soft dough, adding the rest of the milk if the mixture is too dry; it should be soft and slightly sticky.

4. Knead lightly and roll out to a 2 cm (¾ inch) thickness. Cut out rounds, using a 5 cm (2 inch) cutter. Place on the baking sheet and brush the tops with the beaten egg. Bake for 10-12 minutes until well risen and golden brown. Transfer to a wire rack to cool. Serve split, with butter, or clotted cream and fruits.

NOTE: Use either ½ or 1 sachet saffron strands, depending on the strength of flavour required. As with any recipe using baking powder, scones should be baked immediately as the baking powder is activated as soon as it comes into contact with liquids.

ORANGE AND ROSEMARY SCONES

Replace the saffron with the finely grated rind of 1 orange and 15 ml (1 tbsp) finely snipped rosemary leaves. Do not heat the milk before mixing.

TECHNIQUE

Roll out the dough to a 2 cm (¾ inch) thickness and cut out rounds, using a 4 cm (1½ inch) pastry cutter. Re-roll trimmings and cut out more rounds.

FLORENTINES

These enticing chewy morsels are rich with fruit and nuts, and this original version also includes sunflower seeds. After baking, the edges of the florentines are rolled in melted chocolate. As an alternative, spread the chocolate over the backs of the biscuits and mark into wavy lines with a fork.

MAKES 12

25 g (1 oz) glacé cherries
40 g (1½ oz) flaked almonds
60 g (2½ oz) unsalted butter
50 g (2 oz) caster sugar
30 ml (2 tbsp) double cream
25 g (1 oz) sunflower seeds
20 g (¾ oz) chopped mixed
   peel
20 g (¾ oz) sultanas
15 g (½ oz) plain white flour
125 g (4 oz) plain dark
   chocolate, in pieces

PREPARATION TIME
15 minutes
COOKING TIME
8-10 minutes
FREEZING
Not suitable

170 CALS PER BISCUIT

I. Preheat the oven to 180°C (350°F) Mark 4. Lightly grease a large baking sheet. Roughly chop the cherries. Lightly crush the almonds.

2. Melt the butter in a small saucepan. Add the sugar and heat gently until dissolved, then bring to the boil. Remove from the heat and stir in the cream, sunflower seeds, mixed peel, sultanas, cherries, almonds and flour. Beat well until evenly combined.

3. Place heaped teaspoonfuls of the mixture onto the baking sheet, spacing them well apart to allow room for spreading. (You'll probably need to cook half the mixture at a time.)

4. Bake for about 6-8 minutes until the biscuits have spread considerably and the edges are golden brown. Remove from the oven and, using a large plain metal biscuit cutter, push the edges into the centre to create neat rounds. Return to the oven for a further 2 minutes or until deep golden.

5. Leave the Florentines on the baking sheet for 2 minutes to cool slightly, then transfer to a wire rack to cool completely. Cook the remaining mixture in the same way.

6. Melt the chocolate in a heatproof bowl over a pan of simmering water. Stir until smooth. Roll the edges of the biscuits in the chocolate and place on a sheet of non-stick baking parchment until set. Store in an airtight tin.

NOTE: If the biscuits solidify before you've had the chance to shape them with the cutter, return to the oven for a further 30 seconds.

VARIATION

For added colour, dip half the biscuits in plain chocolate and the other half in milk or white chocolate.

TECHNIQUE

Working quickly bring the spread edges of the biscuits in to the centre, using a large metal cutter. Finish by rotating the cutter in a circular movement to give perfectly round biscuits.

SPICE FINGER BISCUITS

Crisp and light with a slightly chewy centre, these simple finger biscuits have an almost meringue-like texture. The deliciously spicy after-taste is accentuated by the sprinkling of black pepper, although this can be omitted for a more conventional biscuit. Serve with coffee, or as an accompaniment to creamy desserts.

MAKES 16-18

1 egg white
10 ml (2 tsp) cornflour
2.5 ml (½ tsp) ground
   cinnamon
2.5 ml (½ tsp) ground ginger
125 g (4 oz) caster sugar
75 g (3 oz) ground almonds
freshly ground black pepper
   and extra spice, for
   sprinkling

PREPARATION TIME
12 minutes
COOKING TIME
15 minutes
FREEZING
Not suitable

65-50 CALS PER BISCUIT

1. Preheat the oven to 180°C (350°F) Mark 4. Line a large baking sheet with non-stick baking parchment.

2. Whisk the egg white in a bowl until stiff, but not dry. Sift the cornflour and spices over the egg white. Add the sugar and ground almonds and gently stir the ingredients together to form a light sticky paste.

3. Place the mixture in a large piping bag, fitted with a 1 cm (½ inch) plain nozzle. Pipe 7 cm (3 inch) finger lengths onto the baking sheet, spacing them slightly apart. Sprinkle with pepper and a little extra spice and bake for 12 minutes or until crisp and golden. Transfer to a wire rack to cool.

NOTE: If you don't have a suitable piping nozzle, spoon walnut-sized pieces of the mixture onto the lined baking sheet instead.

VARIATIONS

Coriander Biscuits: Substitute ground coriander for the cinnamon and add the grated rind of ½ orange. Sprinkle crushed coriander over the biscuits before baking.
Coconut Biscuits: Replace the spices and ground almonds with 75 g (3 oz) desiccated coconut and add a few drops of almond essence.

TECHNIQUE

Pipe 7.5 cm (3 inch) finger lengths of the mixture onto the lined baking sheet, using a knife to break off the mixture.

ALMOND FUDGE CRUMBLES

Hidden pieces of crushed almond flakes and chewy fudge marry perfectly in these simple biscuits. Scattered with more crumbled fudge and almonds, they are baked to a cookie-like crumbliness, then served with a dusting of icing sugar. Choose a good quality almond essence to bring out the full almond flavour.

MAKES 24

75 g (3 oz) flaked almonds
50 g (2 oz) vanilla fudge
200 g (7 oz) plain white flour
pinch of salt
2.5 ml (½ tsp) bicarbonate of
   soda
125 g (4 oz) unsalted butter
125 g (4 oz) muscovado
   sugar
I egg
5 ml (I tsp) almond essence
TOPPING
25 g (I oz) flaked almonds
25 g (I oz) vanilla fudge
icing sugar, for dusting

PREPARATION TIME
10 minutes
COOKING TIME
12 minutes
FREEZING
Suitable

130 CALS PER BISCUIT

I. Preheat the oven to 190°C (375°F) Mark 5. Lightly grease two baking sheets. Crumble the almonds into small flakes. Finely dice the fudge.

2. Sift the flour, salt and bicarbonate of soda into a bowl. Add the butter, cut into small pieces, and rub in using the fingertips. Add the sugar, egg, almond essence, flaked almonds and fudge and mix to a fairly firm dough.

3. Turn onto a lightly floured surface and roll into a cylinder, 23 cm (9 inches) long. Cut the dough into 24 rounds. Place the rounds, slightly apart, on the baking sheets.

4. Lightly crumble the almonds and chop the fudge for the topping. Scatter over the biscuits and press down lightly to adhere. Bake the biscuits for about 12 minutes until turning golden around the edges. Leave on the baking sheets for 5 minutes, then transfer to a wire rack to cool. Serve dusted with icing sugar.

NOTE: Use a slab of vanilla or 'cream' fudge, or individually wrapped sweets.

VARIATIONS

Coffee and Walnut Crumbles: Add 15 ml (I tbsp) finely ground espresso coffee to the dry ingredients and substitute finely ground walnuts for the almonds.

Apple and Raisin Crumbles: Use raisin fudge and substitute chopped dried apples for half of the almonds.

TECHNIQUE

Cut the cylinder of dough into 24 equal-sized pieces.

DOUBLE CHOCOLATE COOKIES

Chunky, crumbly and rich with chocolate, these delicious biscuits closely resemble home-baked American style cookies. This quick, simple recipe – with its generous proportions of dark and white chocolate – is guaranteed to appeal to all chocolate lovers.

MAKES 18

125 g (4 oz) white chocolate
125 g (4 oz) plain dark
   chocolate
125 g (4 oz) unsalted butter,
   softened
125 g (4 oz) caster sugar
1 egg
5 ml (1 tsp) vanilla essence
125 g (4 oz) porridge oats
150 g (5 oz) plain white flour
2.5 ml (½ tsp) baking
   powder

PREPARATION TIME
15 minutes
COOKING TIME
12-15 minutes
FREEZING
Suitable

215 CALS PER BISCUIT

1. Preheat the oven to 180°C (350°F) Mark 4. Lightly grease two baking sheets. Chop the white and plain chocolate into small chunks, each no larger than 1 cm (½ inch) in diameter.

2. Put the butter and sugar in a bowl and beat until creamy and paler in colour. Add the egg, vanilla essence and oats. Sift the flour and baking powder into the bowl and mix until evenly combined. Stir in the chocolate.

3. Place dessertspoonfuls of the mixture on the prepared baking sheets, spacing them well apart to allow room for spreading. Flatten slightly with the back of a fork.

4. Bake for 12-15 minutes until risen and turning golden. Leave on the baking sheets for 5 minutes, then transfer to a wire rack to cool. Store in an airtight tin for up to 1 week.

NOTE: The cookies will only become firm as they cool. Don't be tempted to bake them until crisp.

VARIATIONS

Toasted Pine Nut Cookies: Cream an extra 25 g (1 oz) sugar with the butter. Replace the chocolate with 40 g (1½ oz) toasted pine nuts. Sprinkle the tops with a further 15 g (½ oz) pine nuts.

Triple Chocolate Cookies: Replace 15 g (½ oz) flour with cocoa powder.

TECHNIQUE

Place dessertspoonfuls of the mixture, well apart, on the baking sheets, shaping them into fairly compact rounds. Flatten each with the back of a fork.

LEMON AND CARDAMOM RINGS

Cardamom seeds – crushed to extract their heady fragrance and spicy, lemony flavour – are combined with plenty of lemon zest in these attractive biscuit rings. A deliciously tangy, smooth lemon icing is brushed over the tops of the biscuits after baking.

MAKES ABOUT 14

15 ml (1 tbsp) cardamom
    pods
175 g (6 oz) unsalted butter
50 g (2 oz) caster sugar
225 g (8 oz) plain white flour
finely grated rind of
    2 lemons
20-25 ml (4-5 tsp) lemon
    juice

LEMON ICING
125 g (4 oz) icing sugar
25-35 ml (5-7 tsp) lemon
    juice

TO DECORATE
15 ml (1 tbsp) cardamom
    pods
strips of finely pared lemon
    rind, for sprinkling

PREPARATION TIME
20 minutes, plus chilling
COOKING TIME
10-12 minutes
FREEZING
Not suitable

170 CALS PER BISCUIT

1. Preheat the oven to 180°C (350°F) Mark 4. Lightly grease two baking sheets. Crush the cardamom pods, using a pestle and mortar, to remove the seeds. Discard the pods and lightly crush the seeds.

2. Cream the butter and sugar together in a bowl until pale and fluffy. Beat in the flour, cardamom seeds, lemon rind and enough lemon juice to mix to a smooth paste.

3. Place half of the mixture in a piping bag, fitted with a 1 cm (½ inch) plain nozzle. Pipe a small round of paste onto a baking sheet. Continue piping adjacent small rounds to shape a ring. Repeat with the remaining paste to make about 14 rings. Chill in the refrigerator for about 30 minutes.

4. Bake the biscuits for 10-12 minutes until turning golden around the edges. Transfer to a wire rack to cool.

5. To make the icing, sift the icing sugar into a bowl and mix in enough lemon juice to give the consistency of pouring cream. Brush over the tops of the biscuits. Crush more cardamom seeds, as above, and sprinkle over the biscuits with the lemon rind.

NOTE: Use a lemon zester to pare delicate strips of rind for decoration. Alternatively finely grate the rind.

VARIATIONS

Use grated orange or lime rind and juice in place of the lemon.

TECHNIQUE

Pipe small adjacent rounds of the mixture in circles to form biscuit rings, about 7.5 cm (3 inches) in diameter.

CHOCOLATE SOFT CENTRES

These crackled, crumbly biscuits consist of a crisp chocolate 'case' which cleverly conceals a velvet smooth chocolate centre. When served freshly baked the filling literally melts in-the-mouth; if served cool it hardens slightly to an equally delicious fudge-like texture.

MAKES 18

150 g (5 oz) unsalted butter, softened
150 g (5 oz) caster sugar
1 egg yolk
25 g (1 oz) cocoa powder
250 g (9 oz) self-raising flour
18-20 squares plain chocolate, about 125 g (4 oz)
TO FINISH
cocoa powder, for dusting

PREPARATION TIME
20 minutes, plus chilling
COOKING TIME
10 minutes
FREEZING
Suitable

180 CALS PER BISCUIT

1. Lightly grease a large baking sheet. Cream the butter and sugar together in a bowl until pale and fluffy. Beat in the egg yolk. Sift the cocoa powder and flour into the bowl and mix to a firm dough, using a round-bladed knife.

2. Turn out onto a lightly floured surface and knead lightly. Chill in the refrigerator for 30 minutes.

3. Preheat the oven to 190°C (375°F) Mark 5. Roll a third of the dough out thinly on a floured surface and cut out 18 circles, using a 4 cm (1½ inch) cutter. Place on the prepared baking sheet and press a chocolate square into the centre of each one.

4. Roll out the remaining dough and cut out 18 larger circles, using a 5 cm (2 inch) cutter. Lay these over the chocolate bases, securing the edges to enclose the chocolate filling.

5. Bake for 10 minutes or until the biscuits have spread and risen. Leave on the baking sheet for 5 minutes, then transfer to a wire rack to cool. Serve dusted with cocoa powder.

NOTE: The larger circles of dough will crack slightly as you position them over the bases.

VARIATION

Use milk or white chocolate squares to fill the biscuits instead of plain chocolate.

TECHNIQUE

Lay the larger circles of dough over the chocolate bases, moulding and easing them to fit.

RASPBERRY AND PISTACHIO SANDWICH CAKE

This all-in-one Victoria sandwich recipe gives excellent results – producing a cake that's light, moist and exceptionally spongy. Pistachio nuts flavour the cake to delicious effect, while fresh raspberries and cream provide an irresistible filling. Make the cake up to a day in advance and assemble an hour or two before serving.

MAKES 8-10 SLICES

65 g (2½ oz) shelled
   pistachio nuts
225 g (8 oz) self-raising
   white flour
10 ml (2 tsp) baking powder
4 eggs
225 g (8 oz) caster sugar
225 g (8 oz) unsalted butter,
   softened
5 ml (1 tsp) vanilla essence
FILLING
125 g (4 oz) raspberries
150 ml (¼ pint) double
   cream, or half yogurt and
   half cream
75 ml (5 tbsp) raspberry jam
TO DECORATE
225 g (8 oz) raspberries
25 g (1 oz) pistachio nuts
icing sugar, for dusting
   (optional)

PREPARATION TIME
20 minutes, plus cooling
COOKING TIME
30 minutes
FREEZING
Suitable: Sponge only

635-510 CALS PER SLICE

1. Preheat the oven to 160°C (325°F) Mark 3. Grease and base-line two 20 cm (8 inch) sandwich tins. Put the pistachio nuts in a bowl and pour on boiling water to cover. Leave for 1 minute, then drain and remove the skins. Finely chop the nuts.

2. Sift the flour and baking powder into a bowl. Add the eggs, sugar, butter and vanilla essence and beat, using an electric whisk, until pale and creamy. Stir in the chopped nuts.

3. Divide the mixture evenly between the tins and level the surfaces. Bake for about 30 minutes until well risen and firm to the touch. Turn out of the tins and leave to cool on a wire rack.

4. Heat the jam in a small pan until just melted; leave to cool. Place one cake layer on a serving plate. Whip the cream until just peaking and spread over the cake. Scatter with the raspberries, then spoon over the melted jam. Top with the second cake layer.

5. To decorate, scatter the raspberries over the cake. Skin the pistachios (as above) and sprinkle over top. Dust with icing sugar if desired, and keep in a cool place until ready to serve.

NOTE: The mixture should be very soft and drop easily from a spoon before baking. If it seems a little stiff, stir in a dash of milk or water.

VARIATION

Replace the pistachio nuts with the scooped-out pulp from 3 passion fruit. Replace the raspberries on top of the cake with wedges of fig and seedless black grapes. Scatter the cake with more passion fruit pulp.

TECHNIQUE

Drain the soaked pistachio nuts and place on a tea-towel. Rub firmly to remove the skins.

Vanilla kugelhupf with spice butter

Rich and sweet, with a lovely moist texture, this delicious buttery yeasted cake is quite similar to a brioche. To enhance its subtle flavouring of vanilla sugar, glacé cherries and citrus peel, the kugelhupf is served sliced and lavishly spread with melting spice butter.

MAKES 10 SLICES

25 g (1 oz) glacé cherries
125 g (4 oz) unsalted butter
250 g (9 oz) plain white flour
pinch of salt
10 ml (2 tsp) fast-action
    dried yeast
40 g (1½ oz) caster sugar
15 g (½ oz) vanilla sugar
grated rind of 1 lemon
50 g (2 oz) chopped mixed
    peel
45 ml (3 tbsp) milk
3 eggs
icing sugar, for dusting
SPICE BUTTER
75 g (3 oz) unsalted butter,
    softened
15 ml (1 tbsp) icing sugar
1.25 ml (¼ tsp) ground
    nutmeg
2.5 ml (½ tsp) ground mixed
    spice
1.25 ml (¼ tsp) ground
    ginger

PREPARATION TIME
15 minutes, plus rising
COOKING TIME
25-30 minutes
FREEZING
Suitable

295 CALS PER SLICE

1. Finely chop the cherries. Melt the butter and leave to cool slightly. Sift the flour and salt into a bowl. Add the yeast, sugars, lemon rind, chopped peel and cherries.

2. Beat the melted butter with the milk and eggs. Add to the bowl and beat well for 2 minutes. Cover the bowl with cling film and leave in a warm place until the mixture has doubled in size.

3. Meanwhile make the spice butter. Beat the ingredients together in a bowl until thoroughly combined. Turn into a small serving dish and keep in a cool place.

4. Preheat the oven to 200°C (400°F) Mark 6. Brush a 20 cm (8 inch) kugelhupf tin or 1.7 litre (3 pint) ring tin with a little melted white vegetable fat. Dust with flour and shake out excess.

5. Lightly beat the risen dough to reduce the volume, then turn into the prepared tin. Cover with oiled cling film and leave to rise until the dough almost reaches the top of the tin.

6. Bake the kugelhupf for 25-30 minutes until deep golden. Leave in the tin for 5 minutes, then loosen the edges with a knife. Invert tin onto a wire rack and tap

the cake out. Cool slightly before serving, dusted with icing sugar and accompanied by the spiced butter.

NOTE: Although very easy to make, you need to allow plenty of time for the dough to rise. This might take 2 hours for the first proving and a further 1 hour in the tin.

VANILLA SUGAR

To make your own vanilla sugar, simply bury a vanilla pod in a jar of caster sugar and leave it for about 2 weeks before using the sugar. If you haven't any vanilla sugar to hand, replace with ordinary caster sugar and add a generous splash of pure vanilla essence.

TECHNIQUE

Once the dough has doubled in size and is spongy in texture, beat well to reduce the volume.

CARROT CAKE WITH MASCARPONE TOPPING

In this carrot cake, brazil nuts replace the more familiar walnuts and mild, creamy mascarpone provides a delicious smooth frosting. The crowning glory is a rich decoration of fried carrot shavings – crisp, golden and lightly sugared. You could, of course, apply a sprinkling of chopped toasted nuts instead.

MAKES 8-10 SLICES

350 g (12 oz) carrots
125 g (4 oz) brazil nuts
225 g (8 oz) unsalted butter
    or margarine, softened
225 g (8 oz) caster sugar
175 g (6 oz) self-raising
    white flour
5 ml (1 tsp) baking powder
2.5 ml (½ tsp) ground allspice
4 eggs
grated rind of 1 orange
15 ml (1 tbsp) orange juice
50 g (2 oz) ground almonds
FROSTING
250 g (9 oz) mascarpone or
    low-fat cream cheese
5 ml (1 tsp) finely grated
    orange rind (optional)
30 ml (2 tbsp) orange juice
30 ml (2 tbsp) icing sugar
TO DECORATE
1 large carrot
oil, for frying
icing sugar, for dusting

PREPARATION TIME
25 minutes, plus cooling
COOKING TIME
35-40 minutes
FREEZING
Suitable: Cake only

735-570 CALS PER SLICE

1. Preheat the oven to 180°C (350°F) Mark 4. Grease and base-line two 18 cm (7 inch) base measurement moule à manque tins or sandwich tins. Dust the sides of the tins with flour and shake out the excess. Peel and finely grate the carrots. Coarsely chop the Brazil nuts and lightly toast them.

2. Cream the butter or margarine and sugar together in a bowl until pale and fluffy. Sift the flour, baking powder and allspice into the bowl. Add the eggs, orange rind and juice, and the ground almonds; beat well. Stir in the carrots and brazil nuts.

3. Divide the mixture between the tins and level the surfaces. Bake for 35-40 minutes until risen and firm to touch. Transfer to a wire rack to cool.

4. For the topping, beat the cheese, orange rind if using, orange juice and icing sugar together in a bowl until smooth. Use half to sandwich the cakes together. Spread the remainder over the top of the cake, swirling it attractively.

5. For the decoration, peel the carrot and pare into long thin ribbons, using a swivel vegetable peeler. Dry the carrot ribbons on kitchen paper. Heat a 1 cm (½ inch) depth of oil in a frying pan until a piece of carrot added to the hot oil sizzles on the surface. Fry the carrots, in two batches, until they shrink and turn golden. Drain with a slotted spoon and dry on kitchen paper.

6. Scatter the carrot pieces over the top of the cake and dust with icing sugar. Chill until ready to serve.

NOTE: It is important to thoroughly dry the carrot ribbons before frying to ensure a crisp result.

TECHNIQUE

Fry the carrot ribbons, half at a time, in the hot oil. When shrivelled and turning golden, lift out with a slotted spoon and transfer to kitchen paper to dry and crisp.

CHOCOLATE PECAN FUDGE CAKE

Layers of dark, moist chocolate cake are sandwiched together with a filling of whipped cream, toasted pecan nuts and sweet maple syrup, then lavishly swirled with an irresistible chocolate fudge icing. Piled high with chocolate curls, this cake really is the ultimate taste in chocolate.

MAKES 16 SLICES

175 g (6 oz) self-raising white flour
50 g (2 oz) cocoa powder
10 ml (2 tsp) baking powder
175 g (6 oz) butter or margarine, softened
175 g (6 oz) caster sugar
4 eggs
10 ml (2 tsp) vanilla essence
FILLING
300 ml (½ pint) double cream
125 g (4 oz) shelled pecans
90 ml (6 tbsp) maple syrup
ICING
300 g (10 oz) plain dark chocolate
50 g (2 oz) unsalted butter
60 ml (4 tbsp) milk
225 g (8 oz) icing sugar
TO DECORATE
200 g (7 oz) plain dark chocolate
cocoa powder, for dusting

PREPARATION TIME
50 minutes, plus cooling
COOKING TIME
25 minutes
FREEZING
Suitable: Without decoration

590 CALS PER SLICE

1. Preheat the oven to 180°C (350°F) Mark 4. Grease and base-line three 19-20 cm (7½ -8 inch) sandwich tins.

2. Sift the flour, cocoa and baking powder into a bowl. Add the butter or margarine, sugar, eggs and vanilla essence. Beat, using an electric whisk, for 2 minutes until smooth and paler in colour. Divide the mixture between the prepared tins and level the surfaces. Bake for 25 minutes until risen and just firm to the touch. Turn out onto a wire rack to cool.

3. For the filling, whip the cream until just peaking. Roughly chop the pecans. Place one cake on a serving plate and spread with a quarter of the cream. Scatter with half of the nuts, then drizzle with half the maple syrup. Spread carefully with another quarter of the cream and position the second cake on top. Cover with the remaining cream, nuts and syrup, then top with the remaining cake.

4. To make the icing, break up the chocolate and place in a saucepan with the butter and milk. Heat gently until the chocolate is melted, stirring frequently. Remove from the heat and beat in the icing sugar until evenly combined. Leave to cool, then swirl over the top and sides of the cake with a palette knife.

5. To make the chocolate curls for the decoration, break up the chocolate and place in a heatproof bowl over a pan of hot water. Leave until melted, then spread evenly onto a marble slab or work surface. When just set draw the blade of a knife, held at a 45° angle, across the chocolate to shave off curls.

6. Scatter the chocolate curls over the top of the cake and dust lightly with cocoa powder.

NOTE: If the chocolate breaks, it has set too hard and should be left in a warm place for a few minutes before trying again.

TECHNIQUE

Draw the blade of a knife, held at a 45° angle, across the chocolate to shave off curls. Adjust the angle of the knife to obtain the best curls.

CRUMBLY APPLE AND CHEESE CAKE

This moist, crumbly fruit cake conceals a layer of tart Caerphilly cheese, which perfectly complements the sweet tang of the dessert apples. Serve while still slightly warm – to accentuate the flavours. Alternatively, you will find that the cake reheats well.

MAKES 10 SLICES

575 g (1¼ lb) dessert apples

50 g (2 oz) brazil nuts

175 g (6 oz) self-raising white flour

5 ml (1 tsp) baking powder

75 g (3 oz) light muscovado sugar

50 g (2 oz) raisins

50 g (2 oz) sultanas

2 eggs

90 ml (3 fl oz) sunflower oil

225 g (8 oz) Caerphilly cheese

TO FINISH

icing sugar, for sprinkling

PREPARATION TIME
20 minutes
COOKING TIME
50 minutes-1 hour
FREEZING
Suitable

345 CALS PER SLICE

1. Preheat the oven to 180°C (350°F) Mark 4. Grease a 5 cm (2 inch) deep, 23 cm (9 inch) round loose-based flan tin. Peel, core and thinly slice the apples. Roughly chop the nuts.

2. Sift the flour and baking powder into a bowl. Stir in the sugar, raisins, sultanas, nuts and apples, and mix until evenly combined. Beat the eggs with the oil and add to the dry ingredients. Stir until all the flour mixture is moistened and evenly incorporated.

3. Turn half the mixture into the prepared tin and level the surface. Crumble the cheese over the surface, then cover with the remaining cake mixture. Roughly spread the mixture to the edges of the tin.

4. Bake for 50 minutes to 1 hour until golden and just firm. Leave to cool in the tin for 10 minutes, then transfer to a wire rack. Serve warm, sprinkled with icing sugar.

NOTE: Do not smooth the second layer of cake mixture too neatly; a rough surface gives a more interesting finish.

VARIATION

Replace the Caerphilly with a similar cheese, such as Wensleydale or Lancashire.

TECHNIQUE

Roughly crumble the cheese over the cake mixture to within 1 cm (½ inch) of the edges.

RIPPLED DATE AND BANANA LOAF

This simple, homely teabread has a beautifully moist texture and a distinctive banana flavour, with a slight tang. Rippled layers of puréed dates provide added interest. To ring the changes, use other dried fruits – such as figs, prunes and apricots – in place of the dates.

MAKES 8-10 SLICES

250 g (9 oz) stoned dried dates
grated rind and juice of 1 lemon
2 ripe bananas
175 g (6 oz) unsalted butter, softened
175 g (6 oz) caster sugar
3 eggs
225 g (8 oz) self-raising white flour
2.5 ml (½ tsp) baking powder

PREPARATION TIME
20 minutes
COOKING TIME
1¼-1½ hours
FREEZING
Suitable

495-395 CALS PER SERVING

1. Preheat the oven to 160°C (325°F) Mark 3. Grease and line a 1.1 litre (2 pint) loaf tin. Set aside 4 dates. Place the remainder in a small heavy-based saucepan and add the lemon rind and juice, and 90 ml (3 fl oz) water. Bring to the boil, reduce the heat and simmer gently for 5 minutes until the dates are soft and pulpy. Purée the mixture in a food processor or blender until smooth. (Alternatively mash together in a bowl, using a fork).

2. Mash the bananas until completely smooth. Cream the butter and sugar together in a bowl until pale and fluffy. Add the banana purée and eggs. Sift the flour and baking powder into the bowl and beat until thoroughly combined.

3. Spoon a third of the banana mixture into the prepared loaf tin and level the surface. Spread half of the date purée over the surface. Repeat these layers, then cover with the remaining banana mixture.

4. Cut the reserved dates into thin lengths and scatter them over the surface. Bake for 1-1¼ hours until well risen and firm to the touch. Leave in the tin for 15 minutes, then transfer to a wire rack to cool. Store in an airtight container for up to 1 week.

NOTE: The date purée needs to be similar in consistency to the banana mixture. If it seems is too thick, beat in a little water.

VARIATIONS

Add 2.5 ml (½ tsp) ground cinnamon or 25 g (1 oz) toasted sunflower seeds to the banana mixture.

TECHNIQUE

Carefully and evenly spread half of the date purée over the banana layer, smoothing it into the corners.

MOIST FRUIT CAKE WITH GLACÉ FRUITS

An impressive arrangement of colourful glacé fruits perfectly offsets this crumbly and exceptionally moist fruit cake. To enhance the moist texture, dried fruits are first simmered in a buttery syrup to plump and sweeten them. Look for quality glacé fruits in good confectioners and specialist food stores – they are well worth the expense! For a less costly alternative, try one of the variations.

MAKES 12 SLICES

200 g (7 oz) dried apple rings
300 g (10 oz) mixed dried fruit
200 g (7 oz) molasses sugar
175 g (6 oz) unsalted butter or margarine
275 ml (9 fl oz) cold black tea
350 g (12 oz) self-raising white flour
5 ml (1 tsp) baking powder
15 ml (1 tbsp) ground mixed spice
1 egg
30 ml (2 tbsp) black treacle
100 g (3½ oz) glacé ginger pieces
TO DECORATE
60 ml (4 tbsp) apricot jam
450 g (1 lb) mixed glacé fruits (pears, plums, cherries, pineapple, etc)

PREPARATION TIME
20 minutes, plus cooling
COOKING TIME
1-1¼ hours
FREEZING
Suitable: Before decorating

515 CALS PER SLICE

1. Preheat the oven to 160°C (325°F) Mark 3. Grease and line a deep 23 cm (9 inch) round cake tin. Roughly chop the apples and place in a saucepan with the other dried fruit, sugar, butter or margarine and tea. Bring to the boil, reduce the heat and simmer gently for 5 minutes. Remove from the heat and leave to cool completely.

2. Sift the flour, baking powder and mixed spice into a bowl. Add the cooled fruit mixture, egg, treacle, ginger and liquid; beat well until the ingredients are evenly combined.

3. Turn the cake mixture into the prepared tin and level the surface. Bake for 1-1¼ hours, or until a skewer inserted in the centre comes out clean. Leave in the tin for 15 minutes, then transfer to a wire rack to cool.

4. To finish the cake, heat the apricot jam in a small saucepan until softened, then press through a sieve into a bowl. Brush a little of the apricot glaze over the cake.

5. Cut any larger pieces of glacé fruit into small wedges or slices. Arrange the fruits over the cake, then brush with the remaining glaze.

NOTE: If more convenient, the dried fruit mixture can be cooked and cooled a day in advance.

VARIATIONS

For a more everyday fruit cake omit the glacé fruit topping. Instead, generously sprinkle the top of the cake with demerara sugar or decorate with whole blanched almonds before baking.

TECHNIQUE

Turn the cake mixture into the prepared tin and level the surface.

STICKY GINGERBREAD

Sticky black treacle and syrupy stem ginger make a perfect partnership in this delicious adaptation of an all-time favourite. Grated cooking apple is added for extra moisture, without detracting from the warm spiciness of the ginger. Once baked, a gloss of ginger syrup adds the finishing touch.

MAKES 12 SLICES

150 g (5 oz) stem ginger
  pieces, plus 45 ml (3 tbsp)
  syrup from jar
1 large cooking apple, about
  225 g (8 oz)
15 ml (1 tbsp) lemon juice
125 g (4 oz) black treacle
125 g (4 oz) golden syrup
175 g (6 oz) molasses or
  dark muscovado sugar
175 g (6 oz) unsalted butter
225 g (8 oz) plain white flour
125 g (4 oz) plain wholemeal
  flour
5 ml (1 tsp) ground mixed
  spice
7.5 ml (1½ tsp) bicarbonate
  of soda
2 eggs

PREPARATION TIME
20 minutes
COOKING TIME
1 hour 20 minutes
FREEZING
Suitable

350 CALS PER SLICE

1. Preheat the oven to 160°C (325°F) Mark 3. Grease and line a deep 18 cm (7 inch) square cake tin. Thinly slice the ginger pieces. Peel, core and quarter the apple; immerse in a bowl of water with the lemon juice added to prevent discolouration.

2. Put the treacle, syrup and sugar in a saucepan. Cut the butter into pieces and add to the pan. Heat gently until the butter melts; leave to cool slightly.

3. Sift the flours, spice and bicarbonate of soda into a bowl. Grate three quarters of the apple into the bowl and toss lightly in the flour. Add the melted mixture, eggs and three quarters of the ginger pieces. Beat well until thoroughly combined.

4. Turn the mixture into the prepared tin, spreading it into the corners. Using a potato peeler, pare the remaining apple into thin slices. Scatter the apple slices and remaining ginger over the surface of the gingerbread and press down lightly into the mixture with the tip of a knife. Bake for 1 hour 20 minutes or until firm to touch. Leave to cool in the tin.

5. Turn out the cake and drizzle the ginger syrup over the surface.

NOTE: Gingerbread will keep well in an airtight tin for up to 1 week. It's best stored for several days before eating.

VARIATION

For a 'hotter' flavour add 10 ml (2 tsp) ground ginger with the mixed spice.

TECHNIQUE

Pour the cooled syrup mixture into the dry ingredients.

APPLE, SULTANA AND CIDER SLICES

Sweet, fragrant dessert apples are an ideal ingredient to enhance a simple sponge. This moist cake is richly filled with apples and sultanas and baked on a puff pastry base. The fruity flavour is intensified by the sliced apple topping. For an added zing, try the delicious cider glaze variation.

MAKES 12 SLICES

225 g (8 oz) puff pastry
3 dessert apples
15 ml (1 tbsp) lemon juice
175 g (6 oz) unsalted butter, softened
175 g (6 oz) caster sugar
125 g (4 oz) self-raising white flour
75 g (3 oz) self-raising wholemeal flour
2.5 ml (½ tsp) baking powder
3 eggs
45 ml (3 tbsp) medium dry cider
50 g (2 oz) sultanas
10 ml (2 tsp) icing sugar
TO FINISH
icing sugar, for sprinkling

PREPARATION TIME
25 minutes
COOKING TIME
1 hour
FREEZING
Suitable: Without glaze

380 CALS PER SERVING

1. Preheat the oven to 200°C (400°F) Mark 6. Lightly dampen a large baking sheet. Roll out the pastry thinly on a lightly floured surface to a 28 cm (11 inch) square and place on baking sheet. Prick all over with a fork and bake for 10 minutes until risen. Reduce the oven temperature to 180°C (350°F) Mark 4.

2. Lightly grease a 23 cm (9 inch) square shallow baking tin. Cut the pastry to fit the base of the tin, then carefully press into position.

3. Peel, core and slice one of the apples. Place in a bowl of water with 5 ml (1 tsp) of the lemon juice. Core and slice the remaining apples and place in a separate bowl with the remaining lemon juice.

4. Cream the butter and sugar together in a bowl until pale and creamy. Sift the flours and baking powder into a bowl. Add the eggs and cider and beat well until smooth. Drain the peeled apple slices and stir into the mixture with the sultanas. Spoon over the pastry and level the surface.

5. Drain the unpeeled apple slices and arrange over the filling. Dust with the icing sugar and bake for 45-50 minutes until just firm. Leave to cool in the tin for 15 minutes.

6. Dust the cake with icing sugar and serve warm, cut into squares.

NOTE: If you don't have a suitable square tin, use a 23 cm (9 inch) loose-based round cake tin instead.

VARIATION

Instead of dusting with icing sugar, apply a cider-flavoured glaze. Sift 125 g (4 oz) icing sugar into a bowl and stir in 30 ml (2 tbsp) cider to make a smooth icing. Pour over the warm cake, leaving some of the apple slices exposed.

TECHNIQUE

Arrange the well-drained apple slices over the surface of the mixture.

SESAME PRUNE SLICES

Here deliciously sweet, sticky prunes are sandwiched between a buttery shortbread base and a moist, syrupy oatmeal layer. At least you can take comfort from the proportion of healthy ingredients in this tempting traybake! To ring the changes, try using other dried fruits, such as apricots, figs or dates.

MAKES 16 SLICES

BASE
175 g (6 oz) plain white flour
125 g (4 oz) unsalted butter
  or margarine
50 g (2 oz) caster sugar
FILLING
225 g (8 oz) no-need-to-soak
  dried prunes
15 g (½ oz) dark muscovado
  sugar
2.5 ml (½ tsp) cornflour
TOPPING
125 g (4 oz) unsalted butter
  or margarine
75 g (3 oz) caster sugar
15 ml (1 tbsp) honey
125 g (4 oz) no-need-to-soak
  dried prunes
125 g (4 oz) self-raising
  white flour
2.5 ml (½ tsp) bicarbonate of
  soda
125 g (4 oz) medium
  oatmeal
50 g (2 oz) sesame seeds

PREPARATION TIME
20 minutes, plus cooling
COOKING TIME
35 minutes
FREEZING
Suitable

295 CALS PER SLICE

1. Preheat the oven to 180°C (350°F) Mark 4. Grease a baking tin measuring 22×29 cm (8½ × 11½ inches) across the top and 19×27 cm (7½×10½ inches) across the base. (Or use a tin with similar dimensions.)

2. To make the base, sift the flour into a bowl. Add the butter or margarine, cut into small pieces, and rub in using the fingertips. Stir in the sugar until the mixture begins to cling together.

3. Turn into the tin and pack the mixture down well with the back of a tablespoon. Bake for 15 minutes until turning golden around the edges.

4. For the filling, roughly chop the prunes and place in a small saucepan with the sugar and 150 ml (¼ pint) water. Bring to the boil, reduce the heat, cover and simmer gently for 10 minutes. Blend the cornflour with 15ml (1 tbsp) water and add to the pan. Cook for 1 minute, stirring until the juices have thickened. Leave to cool slightly, then spread over the shortbread base.

5. For the topping, place the butter or margarine, sugar and honey in a small pan and heat gently until dissolved. Finely chop the prunes and stir into the mixture.

6. Sift the flour and bicarbonate of soda into a bowl. Add the oatmeal and all but

30 ml (2 tbsp) of the sesame seeds. Add the melted mixture and beat until evenly combined.

7. Spoon the topping over the prunes in the tin and level the surface. Bake for 20 minutes or until the topping is golden and slightly risen. Leave to cool in the tin, then cut into bars. Store in an airtight tin for up to 5 days.

NOTE: A food processor is ideal for mixing the base ingredients together, and for finely chopping the prunes before adding them to the topping.

VARIATIONS

Use other plump dried fruit such as apricots, figs or dates instead of prunes. Add a pinch of mixed spice or grated lemon rind to the topping.

TECHNIQUE

Carefully spoon the oatmeal topping into the tin, being careful not to dislodge the prune layer. Level the surface.

SYRUPY SEMOLINA HALVA

Grainy semolina, baked to form a firm sponge base for citrus fruits saturated in spicy syrup, evokes the flavour of near eastern patisserie! Allow the sponge to steep for several hours or overnight in the thick syrup so that the syrup is thoroughly absorbed. Serve accompanied by thick yogurt and strong black coffee.

MAKES 10 SLICES

125 g (4 oz) unsalted butter, softened
125 g (4 oz) light muscovado sugar
grated rind of 1 orange
grated rind of 1 lemon
30 ml (2 tbsp) lemon juice
2 eggs
175 g (6 oz) semolina
5 ml (1 tsp) baking powder
125 g (4 oz) ground almonds
30 ml (2 tbsp) poppy seeds
TO FINISH
2 oranges
2 lemons
300 g (10 oz) caster sugar
300 ml (½ pint) freshly squeezed orange juice
2 cinnamon sticks, halved

PREPARATION TIME
30 minutes
COOKING TIME
30 minutes
FREEZING
Suitable: Cake only

485 CALS PER SLICE

1. Preheat the oven to 220°C (425°F) Mark 7. Grease and base-line a shallow 23 cm (9 inch) square baking tin. Cream the butter and sugar together until pale and fluffy.

2. Add the orange and lemon rind, lemon juice, eggs, semolina, baking powder, ground almonds and poppy seeds. Beat well until evenly mixed, then turn into the prepared tin and level the surface. Bake for about 20 minutes until slightly risen and turning golden. Remove from the oven and leave to cool in the tin. Peel off the paper, then return to the tin.

3. To finish, finely pare the rind from 1 orange and 1 lemon in strips using a citrus zester. Cut away all the white pith from both oranges and lemons, then thinly slice the fruit. Place the sugar in a heavy-based saucepan with the orange juice, cinnamon sticks and pared fruit rind. Heat gently, stirring until the sugar dissolves, then bring to the boil and boil for 3 minutes.

4. Remove the pared fruit rind and cinnamon from the syrup with a slotted spoon and reserve. Pour just over half of the syrup evenly over the surface of the cake. Scatter the fruit slices, pared rind and cinnamon sticks on top.

5. Return the remaining syrup to the heat and cook for another 5 minutes

or until thickened and beginning to caramelise. Pour evenly over the fruit and leave for several hours before cutting. Store in an airtight plastic container for up to 4-5 days.

NOTE: If preferred, you can arrange the decorative fruits in lines to make cutting easier.

TECHNIQUE

Beat the cake ingredients together until thoroughly mixed; the consistency will be fairly thick.

STICKY ORANGE FLAPJACKS

Coated in buttery syrup and golden baked to a chewy, sticky perfection, porridge oats are transformed into a classic teatime favourite. Nutty sunflower seeds and finely pared orange zest are included in this simple recipe – to provide an interesting new twist.

MAKES 18

2 small oranges
250 g (9 oz) unsalted butter
250 g (9 oz) caster sugar
175 g (6 oz) golden syrup
425 g (15 oz) porridge oats
30 ml (2 tbsp) sunflower
   seeds
45 ml (3 tbsp) fine-shred
   orange marmalade

PREPARATION TIME
10 minutes
COOKING TIME
25-30 minutes
FREEZING
Suitable

300 CALS PER FLAPJACK

1. Preheat the oven to 180°C (350°F) Mark 4. Grease a baking tin measuring 22 × 9 cm (8½ × 11½ inches) across the top and 19 × 27 cm (7½ × 10½ inches) across the base. (Or use a tin with similar dimensions.)

2. Using a citrus zester, finely pare the rind from the oranges in strips. Place in a heavy-based saucepan. Add the butter, cut into pieces, with the sugar and syrup. Cook over a moderate heat, stirring until the butter has melted. Remove from the heat and stir in the oats, until evenly coated in syrup.

3. Turn the mixture into the prepared tin and level the surface. Sprinkle with the sunflower seeds. Bake for 25-30 minutes until turning deep golden around the edges; the mixture will still be very soft in the centre. Leave in the tin until almost cold.

4. Heat the marmalade in a small saucepan with 15 ml (1 tbsp) water until syrupy. Brush evenly over the flapjack. Turn out onto a board and cut into 18 bars. Store in an airtight container for up to 1 week.

NOTE: To weigh syrup, first measure out the sugar quantity and leave it in the scales bowl, making a small well in the centre. Add additional weights for the required quantity of syrup and spoon the syrup into the well. Both sugar and syrup will then slide cleanly into the saucepan.

VARIATIONS

Fruit and Nut Flapjacks: Omit the orange rind, sunflower seeds and marmalade. Add 125 g (4 oz) luxury mixed dried fruit and 75 g (3 oz) chopped and toasted mixed nuts with the oats.

Pear and Cinnamon Flapjacks: Omit the orange rind, sunflower seeds and marmalade. Add 5 ml (1 tsp) ground cinnamon with the sugar, and 150 g (5 oz) roughly chopped dried pears with the oats.

TECHNIQUE

Place the citrus zester against the orange skin and draw firmly towards you to remove the rind in fine strips. Repeat all over the skin.

CHERRY STREUSEL SLICE

Crumbly, mildly spiced and pleasantly sweet, this mouth-watering cake is reminiscent of a traditional fruit crumble. The generous filling of cherries in a syrupy vanilla sauce is encased in a buttery, almond crumble mixture and sprinkled with a similar topping. Serve sliced – preferably with spoonfuls of lightly whipped cream – as a teatime treat, or dessert if you prefer.

MAKES 8 SLICES

two 425 g (15 oz) cans
   pitted black or red
   cherries
10 ml (2 tsp) cornflour
5 ml (1 tsp) vanilla essence
250 g (9 oz) self-raising flour
5 ml (1 tsp) ground
   cinnamon
grated rind of ½ lemon
175 g (6 oz) unsalted butter
165 g (5½ oz) caster sugar
50 g (2 oz) ground almonds
1 egg
icing sugar, for dusting

PREPARATION TIME
20 minutes, plus cooling
COOKING TIME
40-45 minutes
FREEZING
Suitable

480 CALS PER SLICE

1. Drain the cherries, reserving 90 ml (3 fl oz) of the juice. Blend a little of the juice with the cornflour in a small pan. Add the remaining juice and vanilla essence and bring to the boil, stirring. Add the cherries and cook, stirring, for a further 1 minute until thickly coated in the syrup. Leave to cool.

2. Grease a 1.5 litre (2½ pint) loaf tin. Line the base and long sides with a double thickness of greaseproof paper, allowing it to overhang the sides of the tin. Preheat the oven to 180°C (350°F) Mark 4.

3. Place the flour, cinnamon and lemon rind in a food processor. Add the butter, cut into small pieces, and work until the mixture starts to cling together. Add the sugar and ground almonds, and process briefly until the mixture resembles a coarse crumble. (Alternatively rub the butter into the flour, using your fingertips, then stir in the sugar and ground almonds.) Weigh 150 g (5 oz) of the crumble and set aside for the topping. Add the egg to the remaining mixture and mix to a fairly soft paste.

4. Use half the paste to thickly line the base of the tin. Roll out the remainder and cut strips, about 2.5 cm (1 inch) wide. Use these to line the sides of the tin, pressing them to fit around the corners and base, eliminating the joins.

5. Spoon the cherry filling into the centre and sprinkle evenly with the reserved crumble. Bake for 40-45 minutes until the topping is pale golden. Leave in the tin to cool.

6. Loosen the edges at the ends of the tin, then carefully lift out the cake, using the greaseproof paper. Serve dusted with icing sugar.

VARIATIONS

Use fresh or canned stoned plums, or apples slices layered with sultanas, in place of the cherries.

TECHNIQUE

Add the diced butter to the dry ingredients in the food processor and work until the mixture resembles crumbs and starts to cling together.

WHITE CHOCOLATE BROWNIES

Deliciously moist, laden with chocolate and crusted in a glossy coat of sugar, chocolate brownies are one of the most adorabie teatime treats! This white chocolate version, packed with hazelnuts and generous chunks of creamy white chocolate, make an exciting and equally enticing alternative.

MAKES 12

175 g (6 oz) shelled
   hazelnuts
500 g (1 lb 2 oz) white
   chocolate
75 g (3 oz) butter
3 eggs
175 g (6 oz) caster sugar
175 g (6 oz) self-raising
   white flour
pinch of salt
5 ml (1 tsp) vanilla essence

PREPARATION TIME
20 minutes
COOKING TIME
30-35 minutes
FREEZING
Suitable

490 CALS PER BROWNIE

1. Preheat the oven to 190°C (375°F) Mark 5. Grease and line a baking tin measuring 22 × 29 cm (8½ × 11½ inches) across the top and 19 × 27 cm (7½ × 10½ inches) across the base. (Or use a tin with similar dimensions.)

2. Roughly chop the hazelnuts. Roughly chop 400 g (14 oz) of the chocolate and set aside. Break up the remaining chocolate and put into a heatproof bowl with the butter. Place over a pan of simmering water until melted. Leave to cool slightly.

3. Whisk the eggs and sugar together in a large bowl until smooth, then gradually beat in the melted chocolate mixture. Sift the flour and salt over the mixture, then fold in with the hazelnuts, chopped chocolate and vanilla essence.

4. Turn the mixture into the prepared tin and level the surface. Bake for 30-35 minutes until risen and golden, and the centre is just firm to the touch. Leave to cool in the tin. Turn out and cut into 12 squares. Store in an airtight container for up to 1 week.

NOTE: When cooked, the mixture will still be very soft under the crust; it firms up during cooling.

VARIATIONS

Use any other roughly chopped nuts instead of the hazelnuts. Almond, walnuts, pecans and brazil nuts are suitable.

TECHNIQUE

Gradually beat the melted chocolate mixture into the eggs and sugar; the consistency will become quite firm.

APPLE AND BLACKBERRY SCONE

Here the classic combination of tangy apples and flavourful fresh blackberries excels once again. A simple scone – flavoured with just a hint of cinnamon – envelopes the fruit filling, capturing the delicious juices. Serve just warm with spoonfuls of barely whipped cream, as a more-ish teatime treat – or pudding if you prefer.

MAKES 6 SLICES

I cooking apple, about 175 g
    (6 oz)
25 g (I oz) caster sugar
8 cloves
75 g (3 oz) blackberries
10 ml (2 tsp) cornflour
200 g (7 oz) self-raising
    white flour
pinch of salt
2.5 ml (½ tsp) ground
    cinnamon
5 ml (I tsp) baking powder
75 g (3 oz) unsalted butter
25 g (I oz) medium oatmeal
50 g (2 oz) light muscovado
    sugar
90 ml (3 fl oz) milk
TO FINISH
milk, to glaze
demerara sugar and
    medium oatmeal, for
    sprinkling
75 g (3 oz) blackberries

PREPARATION TIME
15 minutes
COOKING TIME
50 minutes
FREEZING
Suitable

300 CALS PER SLICE

1. Preheat the oven to 200°C (400°F) Mark 6. Lightly grease a 19-20 cm (7½-8 inch) spring-release cake tin. Peel, core and thinly slice the apple. Place in a bowl with the sugar, cloves, blackberries and cornflour; toss gently to mix.

2. Sift the flour, salt, cinnamon and baking powder together and place in a food processor. Add the butter, cut into small pieces, and work until the mixture resembles breadcrumbs. Add the oatmeal and sugar. Add most of the milk and process briefly to a soft dough, adding the remaining milk if the mixture is too dry.

3. On a floured surface, roll out two thirds of the dough to a round about 23 cm (9 inches) in diameter. Use to line the tin, so that the dough comes about 2.5 cm (I inch) up the sides. Pile the apple and blackberry mixture into the centre and brush the edges of the dough with a little milk.

4. Roll out the remaining dough to a 19-20 cm (7½-8 inch) round and lay over the filling, pressing the edges gently together to secure.

5. Brush the top with milk. Sprinkle with the demerara sugar and oatmeal and bake for 30 minutes until well risen

and golden. Reduce the oven temperature to 160°C (325°F) Mark 3.

6. Scatter the scone with the remaining blackberries and sprinkle with more sugar and oatmeal. Return to the oven for a further 20 minutes, covering with foil if the scone appears to be over-browning. Leave in the tin for 5 minutes, then transfer to a wire rack to cool.

VARIATIONS

Use pears (preferably the cooking variety) in place of apple. Alternatively, use peaches and substitute raspberries for the blackberries. Frozen blackberries can be used, but they will result in a slightly wetter consistency.

TECHNIQUE

Fit the scone dough into the tin, pressing it into the corners and 2.5 cm (I inch) up the side of the tin.

CHOCOLATE LEAF GÂTEAU

For this stunning gâteau a light, chocolate genoese is split and generously filled with a white chocolate and Cointreau-flavoured cream, then topped with a glossy dark chocolate cream icing and crowned with chocolate leaves. Use a variety of well-defined leaves to make the decoration – for optimum effect.

MAKES 14 SLICES

50 g (2 oz) unsalted butter
5 eggs
150 g (5 oz) caster sugar
125 g (4 oz) plain white flour
25 g (1 oz) cocoa powder
FILLING
200 g (7 oz) white chocolate
300 ml (½ pint) double
   cream
75 ml (5 tbsp) Cointreau or
   other orange-flavoured
   liqueur
ICING
225 g (8 oz) plain dark
   chocolate, in pieces
225 g (8 oz) double cream
TO DECORATE
75 g (3 oz) bitter chocolate
75 g (3 oz) plain dark
   chocolate
75 g (3 oz) milk chocolate
selection of clean, dry
   leaves, such as rose, large
   mint, lemon geranium
   and small bay leaves

PREPARATION TIME
1½ hours, plus cooling
COOKING TIME
30 minutes
FREEZING
Suitable: Before icing

560 CALS PER SLICE

1. Preheat the oven to 180°C (350°F) Mark 4. Grease and line a 23 cm (9 inch) spring-release cake tin. Melt the butter in a saucepan; leave to cool slightly.

2. Put the eggs and sugar in a large heatproof bowl standing over a pan of hot water. Whisk until pale and creamy, and thick enough to leave a trail on the surface when the whisk is lifted.

3. Remove from the heat and whisk until cool. Sift together the flour and cocoa powder, then fold half into the egg mixture using a metal spoon. Pour the butter around the edge of the mixture and lightly fold in. Gradually fold in the remaining flour and cocoa.

4. Pour into the tin. Bake for about 30 minutes until well risen, just firm to touch and beginning to shrink from sides of tin. Turn out and cool on a wire rack.

5. To make the filling, finely grate the white chocolate. Whip cream with the liqueur until thickened but not peaking. Fold in the chocolate. Split the sponge horizontally and sandwich together with the cream. Invert onto a wire rack so that the flat base is now the top.

6. For the icing, place the chocolate in a heavy-based saucepan with the cream. Heat gently until chocolate is almost melted. Remove from heat and stir until smooth and glossy; let cool slightly.

7. Position a large plate or tray under the wire rack holding the cake. Pour the icing onto the cake. Using a palette knife, ease the icing down the side until the cake is completely covered. Carefully transfer to a serving plate.

8. For the chocolate leaves, break up the bitter chocolate and place in a heatproof bowl over a pan of hot water and leave until melted. Repeat with the plain and milk chocolate; keep separate.

9. Using a paintbrush, paint the undersides of the leaves with the different melted chocolates, taking it just to the edges. (You'll need about 15 of each shade). Leave in a cool place or refrigerate until set. Carefully peel the leaves away from the chocolate. Press the chocolate leaves gently around the sides of the gâteau to decorate.

TECHNIQUE

Once all of the icing has been poured over the top of the cake, ease it down the side, spreading with a palette knife.

COCONUT GÂTEAU WITH LIME AND KIRSCH

This beautiful white sponge is made using a meringue base into which the dry ingredients and flavourings are folded. Lime zest speckles the sponge and a kirsch syrup gives a moist kick. Freshly toasted coconut shavings and syrupy lime slices add both sweetness and tang to the rich cream coating.

MAKES 10-12 SLICES

7 egg whites
good pinch of salt
5 ml (1 tsp) cream of tartar
10 ml (2 tsp) vanilla essence
300 g (10 oz) caster sugar
finely grated rind of 2 limes
50 g (2 oz) freshly grated
  coconut, or desiccated
  coconut
125 g (4 oz) plain white flour
TO ASSEMBLE
4 limes
50 g (2 oz) caster sugar
60 ml (4 tbsp) kirsch
125 g (4 oz) piece fresh
  coconut, or coconut
  shreds
450 ml (¾ pint) double
  cream
45 ml (3 tbsp) icing sugar
175 g (6 oz) Greek-style
  yogurt

PREPARATION TIME
45 minutes, plus cooling
COOKING TIME
30 minutes
FREEZING
Suitable: Cake only

515-430 CALS PER SLICE

1. Preheat the oven to 160°C (325°F) Mark 3. Grease and base-line two 20 cm (8 inch) sandwich tins. Whisk the egg whites in a large bowl until just holding their shape. Add the salt and cream of tartar and whisk until stiff but not dry. Gradually whisk in the sugar, a little at a time, whisking well between each addition until stiff and very shiny. Whisk in the lime rind with the last of the sugar.

2. Add the coconut, then sift in the flour and lightly fold in until just incorporated. Divide between the tins and level the surfaces. Bake for 30 minutes until the surfaces are pale golden and crusty. Leave to cool in the tins.

3. For the decoration, finely pare the rind from two of the limes in shreds, using a sharp knife. Remove the peel and white pith from all 4 limes; thinly slice the flesh. Dissolve the sugar in 150 ml (¼ pint) water in a small heavy-based pan over a low heat. Add the lime slices and shredded rind and cook gently for 1 minute. Drain with a slotted spoon and reserve. Leave the syrup to cool.

4. Stir the kirsch into the cooled syrup. Split each cake in half horizontally and drizzle each layer with the syrup. If using fresh coconut, cut away the skin, then pare the flesh using a swivel vegetable peeler. Lightly toast the parings or coconut shreds until turning golden.

5. Whip the cream with the icing sugar until just peaking, then fold in the yogurt. Place one cake layer on a serving plate and spread with a little of the cream mixture. Arrange a quarter of the lime slices on top and sprinkle with a little of the coconut shavings. Repeat the layers twice, using up half the cream and most of the coconut and lime slices. Top with the final cake layer.

6. Spread the remaining cream all over the cake. Decorate the top with the remaining lime slices and coconut, and the pared lime rind. Chill in the refrigerator until ready to serve.

TECHNIQUE

Using a metal tablespoon, carefully fold the flour and coconut into the meringue mixture until just incorporated.

HAZELNUT MERINGUE GÂTEAU

Tiers of lightly spiced meringue – laced with two-tone chocolate pieces – form a delicious case for lightly whipped cream and a hazelnut praline. For a lighter gâteau, replace half of the cream with thick Greek-style yogurt or fromage frais. You can also increase the amount of spice if you prefer a more intense flavour.

MAKES 10 SLICES

MERINGUE
125 g (4 oz) shelled
   hazelnuts
5 egg whites
250 g (9 oz) caster sugar
2.5 cm (½ tsp) ground mixed
   spice
75 g (3 oz) white chocolate
   chopped
75 g (3 oz) plain chocolate,
   chopped
TO ASSEMBLE
75 g (3 oz) shelled hazelnuts
125 g (4 oz) caster sugar
300 ml (½ pint) double
   cream
cocoa powder, for dusting

PREPARATION TIME
40 minutes, plus cooling
COOKING TIME
About 1½ hours
FREEZING
Not suitable

630 CALS PER SLICE

1. Line 2 baking sheets with non-sticking baking parchment. Draw a 23 cm (9 inch) circle onto one sheet, using a plate as a guide. On the other sheet, draw a 17.5 cm (6½ inch) circle. Turn the paper over. Preheat the oven to 140°C (275°F) Mark 1.

2. To make the meringue, lightly toast the hazelnuts, then chop roughly. Whisk the egg whites in a bowl until stiff but not dry. Gradually whisk in the sugar, a tablespoon at a time, whisking well between each addition until the meringue is stiff and very shiny. Whisk in the spice with the last of the sugar. Carefully fold in the chopped hazelnuts and white and plain chocolate.

3. Spoon the meringue onto the circles, then spread neatly into rounds. Bake for about 1½ hours until dry and the undersides are firm when tapped. Turn the oven off and leave the meringues to cool in the oven.

4. For the praline, lightly oil a baking sheet. Put the hazelnuts in a small heavy-based pan with the sugar. Place over a gentle heat, stirring until the sugar melts. Continue cooking until the mixture caramelises to a rich golden brown colour, then pour onto the baking sheet. Leave to cool and harden.

5. Place the praline in a polythene bag and beat with a rolling pin until very coarsely crushed.

6. Carefully transfer the largest meringue round to a serving plate. Whip the cream until softly peaking, then spread over the meringue. Scatter with the praline. Cover with the smaller meringue round and dust the top of the gâteau with cocoa powder.

NOTE: Remember to switch the baking sheets around halfway through cooking the meringue rounds, to ensure an even result.

TECHNIQUE

Spread the hazelnut meringue onto the prepared baking sheets, just to the edges of the marked circles. Swirl the edges of the large meringue and the whole surface of the smaller meringue with a palette knife.

ALMOND AND APRICOT ROULADE

This irresistible moist roulade is flecked with grated marzipan and drizzled with amaretto liqueur, giving a superb almondy flavour. In perfect contrast, fresh ripe apricots and crème fraîche are encased inside. The roulade is best made a day in advance and filled shortly before serving, preferably with strong dark coffee.

MAKES 8 SLICES

ROULADE
25 g (1 oz) flaked almonds
125 g (4 oz) white almond
   paste
5 eggs, separated
150 g (5 oz) caster sugar
5 ml (1 tsp) vanilla essence
45 ml (3 tbsp) plain flour
45 ml (3 tbsp) amaretto de
   Saronno liqueur
FILLING
6 ripe apricots
300 g (10 oz) crème fraîche
caster or icing sugar, for
   dusting

PREPARATION TIME
20 minutes, plus standing
COOKING TIME
20 minutes
FREEZING
Not suitable

380 CALS PER SLICE

1. Preheat the oven to 180°C (350°F) Mark 4. Grease a 33 × 23 cm (13 × 9 inch) Swiss roll tin and line with greased non-stick baking parchment. Scatter the flaked almonds evenly over the paper. Grate the almond paste.

2. Whisk the egg yolks with 125 g (4 oz) of the sugar until pale and fluffy. Stir in the vanilla essence and grated almond paste. Sift the flour over the mixture, then lightly fold in.

3. Whisk the egg whites in another bowl, until stiff but not dry. Gradually whisk in the remaining sugar. Using a metal tablespoon, carefully fold a quarter of the egg whites into the almond mixture to loosen, then fold in the remainder.

4. Turn into the prepared tin and gently ease the mixture into the corners. Bake for about 20 minutes or until well risen and just firm to the touch. Remove from the oven and cover with a sheet of non-stick baking parchment and a damp tea-towel. Leave until cool, or overnight if possible.

5. Remove the tea-towel and invert the roulade (and paper) onto a baking sheet. Peel off the lining paper. Sprinkle another piece of baking parchment with caster sugar and flip the roulade onto it. Drizzle with the amaretto liqueur.

6. Halve and stone the apricots, then cut into small pieces. Spread the roulade with the crème fraîche and scatter with the apricots. Starting at one of the narrow ends, roll up the roulade. Transfer to a plate and dust with caster or icing sugar to serve.

NOTE: The roulade will probably crack during rolling – this is a characteristic!

VARIATIONS

Replace the apricots with strawberries or raspberries. Brandy or Grand Marnier can be used instead of the amaretto.

TECHNIQUE

Starting from one of the narrow ends, carefully roll up the roulade, using the paper to help.

WALNUT TORTE

The technique of folding whisked egg whites into a creamed mixture gives a soufflé-like quality to this airy sponge, so expect it to deflate slightly after baking. Earthy walnuts and tangy ricotta cheese add a lively, yet not too sweet, flavour that contrasts perfectly with the chocolate decoration.

MAKES 8-10 SLICES

165 g (5½ oz) walnuts
150 g (5 oz) unsalted butter
150 g (5 oz) caster sugar
5 eggs, separated
grated rind of 1 orange
150 g (5 oz) ricotta cheese
40 g (1½ oz) plain white
   flour
TO FINISH
90 ml (6 tbsp) apricot jam
10 ml (2 tsp) orange juice
25 g (1 oz) bitter chocolate,
   in one piece (at room
   temperature)

PREPARATION TIME
25 minutes, plus cooling
COOKING TIME
30 minutes
FREEZING
Not suitable

530-425 CALS PER SLICE

1. Preheat the oven to 190°C (375°F) Mark 5. Grease and base-line of a 23 cm (9 inch) spring-release cake tin. Lightly toast the walnuts, allow to cool, then chop roughly. Set aside 40 g (1½ oz) for the decoration.

2. Cream the butter and 125 g (4 oz) of the sugar together in a bowl until pale and fluffy. Add the egg yolks, orange rind, ricotta cheese, flour and roughly chopped walnuts. Mix gently until evenly combined.

3. Put the egg whites into another large bowl and whisk until stiff but not dry. Gradually whisk in the remaining sugar. Using a metal tablespoon, fold a quarter into the cheese mixture to loosen it slightly, then carefully fold in the remaining egg whites.

4. Turn the mixture into the prepared tin and gently level the surface. Bake for about 30 minutes until risen and just firm. Remove from the oven and leave to cool in the tin.

5. Heat the apricot jam in a pan until melted, then press through a sieve into a bowl and stir in the orange juice to make a glaze.

6. Brush half the apricot glaze around the side of the cake. Using a palette knife, coat the side of the cake with the reserved walnuts.

7. Brush the remaining apricot glaze over the top of the cake. Using a swivel vegetable peeler, shave curls from the chocolate and scatter over the top of the cake to serve.

NOTE: This gâteau can be made in advance and kept in the refrigerator for up to 2 days.

VARIATION

Omit the chocolate curls. Cover the top of the cake with halved and stoned greengages or small plums. Glaze the fruit with 60 ml (4 tbsp) warmed and sieved greengage or plum jam.

TECHNIQUE

Using a palette knife, press the finely chopped nuts around the side of the cake, so that cake and glaze are still partially visible.

TIERED FRUIT GÂTEAU

Tiering a gâteau brings a refreshing informality to any special occasion. In this creation, light sponge layers are sandwiched together with macerated soft fruits and a hazelnut praline cream. Pretty chocolate collars surround the layers, while glazed soft fruits and herb flowers provide the elaborate decoration.

MAKES 24 SLICES

LARGE CAKE
6 eggs
175 g (6 oz) caster sugar
175 g (6 oz) plain white flour
SMALL CAKE
2 eggs
50 g (2 oz) caster sugar
50 g (2 oz) plain white flour
FILLING
350 g (12 oz) strawberries
175 g (6 oz) raspberries
30 ml (2 tbsp) rosewater
40 g (1½ oz) caster sugar
TO FINISH
175 g (6 oz) shelled
   hazelnuts
150 g (5 oz) caster sugar
900 ml (1½ pints) double
   cream
350 g (12 oz) plain chocolate
900 g (2 lb) soft fruits, such
   as strawberries, rasp-
   berries, blueberries, red
   and blackcurrants
105 ml (7 tbsp) redcurrant
   jelly
herb flowers (optional)

PREPARATION TIME
1½ hours, plus cooling
COOKING TIME
45-50 minutes
FREEZING
Suitable: Without glazed fruits

425 CALS PER SLICE

1. Preheat the oven to 180°C (350°F) Mark 4. Grease and base-line a 28 cm (11 inch) and a 15 cm (6 inch) round cake tin. Dust with flour and shake out excess.

2. For the large cake, whisk the eggs and sugar together in a very large heatproof bowl over a pan of hot water until the mixture is thick enough to leave a trail. Remove bowl from pan and whisk until cooled. Sift flour over mixture and fold in lightly. Turn into the large tin and bake for 20-25 minutes until just firm. Cool on a wire rack. Make the small cake in the same way and bake for 15-17 minutes.

3. Slice the strawberries and toss in a bowl with the raspberries, rosewater and sugar. Gently heat the hazelnuts and sugar in a heavy-based pan with 15 ml (1 tbsp) water until sugar dissolves, then cook to a deep brown caramel. Immediately pour onto an oiled baking sheet. Leave to cool and harden, then coarsely crush. Whip the cream until just peaking, then fold in the praline.

4. Halve the cakes horizontally. Sandwich the large cakes together on a platter with two thirds of the fruit filling and a little praline cream. Sandwich the small cake with the remaining fruits and a little more cream. Cut a strip of greaseproof paper, 5 cm (2 inches) longer than the circumference of the large cake and 2 cm (¾ inches) deeper. Repeat for the small cake.

5. Spread remaining praline cream over cakes, then carefully position the small cake, off-centre, on the large one. Chill.

6. Melt the chocolate in a bowl over a pan of simmering water. Spread over each greaseproof strip, right to the long edges and 1 cm (½ inch) from each end. Leave until the chocolate has thickened slightly, then carefully wrap the small strip around the small cake. Wrap the long strip around the large cake (another pair of hands is useful at this point!). Chill for 5-10 minutes until set, then carefully peel away the paper.

7. Decorate the gâteau with the soft fruits. Melt the redcurrant jelly with 15 ml (1 tbsp) water and brush over the fruits. Apply the herb flowers.

TECHNIQUE

Position the small chocolate strip around the small cake, pressing gently to fit.

HOLLY CHRISTMAS CAKE

This simple, elegant Christmas cake is topped with peaked royal icing, and embellished with a colourful ribbon, holly and pine cones. The fruit cake should be set on a much larger platter or board to accommodate the decoration. You will need about 1 metre of 7.5 cm (3 inch) wide ribbon, clean holly leaves and baby fir cones.

MAKES 24 SLICES

75 g (3 oz) glacé cherries
400 g (14 oz) raisins
175 g (6 oz) currants
175 g (6 oz) sultanas
50 g (2 oz) chopped mixed
   peel
45 ml (3 tbsp) brandy
75 g (3 oz) brazil nuts
50 g (2 oz) walnuts
185 g (6½oz) unsalted
   butter
185 g (6½ oz) dark
   muscovado sugar
3 eggs
15 ml (1 tbsp) black treacle
225 g (8 oz) plain white flour
5 ml (1 tsp) ground mixed
   spice
5 ml (1 tsp) ground nutmeg
5 ml (1 tsp) ground cinnamon
TO FINISH
45 ml (3 tbsp) apricot jam
700 g (1½ lb) white almond
   paste
3 egg whites
15 ml (1 tbsp) glycerine
700 g (1½ lb) icing sugar

PREPARATION TIME
1¼ hours, plus cooling
COOKING TIME
3¼-3¾ hours
FREEZING
Suitable: Cake only

505 CALS PER SERVING

1. Preheat the oven to 140°C (275°F) Mark 1. Grease and line a deep 20 cm (8 inch) round cake tin with greased greaseproof paper. Roughly chop the cherries and place in a bowl with the raisins, currants, sultanas, peel and brandy. Stir lightly to combine. Roughly chop the nuts.

2. In a separate bowl, cream the butter and sugar together until pale and fluffy. Gradually beat in the eggs, adding a little of the flour to prevent curdling. Beat in the treacle. Sift the flour and spices over the mixture and fold in, then gently stir in the fruit and nuts.

3. Turn the mixture into the prepared tin and level the surface. Bake for 3¼-3¾ hours or until a skewer inserted in the centre comes out clean. Leave to cool in the tin. Turn out and wrap in a double thickness of foil. Store in a cool, dry place for up to 2 months.

4. To finish the cake, heat the apricot jam until melted, then press through a sieve into a bowl and stir in 15 ml (1 tbsp) hot water. Brush the cake with the glaze and cover with almond paste (see pages 8-9).

5. To make the icing, mix the egg whites, glycerine and a little of the icing sugar in a bowl. Gradually beat in the remaining icing sugar until the icing is stiff and stands in soft peaks.

6. Use a generous half of the icing to cover the side of the cake, spreading with a palette knife to cover evenly. Draw a serrated scraper around the cake to give a decorative finish. Trim off excess icing around the top. Leave to dry for 24 hours.

7. Spread the remaining icing over the top of the cake. Use a palette knife to pull up peaks, letting some overhang the side of the cake. Apply the ribbon, securing with a dot of icing. Surround the cake with holly and fir cones.

NOTE: Keep the surface of the icing tightly covered with cling film when not in use. If storing overnight, rest a damp cloth on the cling film and cover the bowl with a second piece of cling film. Beat lightly before using, adding a little water to loosen if necessary.

TECHNIQUE

Holding the scraper at an angle of about 45°, draw it around the side in one continuous movement.

CELEBRATION CAKE

Delicate garlands of pearl beading make a simple, yet stylish decoration for this stunning celebration cake. Single pearls of icing, subtly dusted with lustre powder, are embossed into the icing below the garlands to complete the effect. Finally, pretty flowers, in soft shades of shell pink and white, are casually assembled on the top of the cake, making the perfect centrepiece for an anniversary, wedding or special birthday gathering.

MAKES 40 SLICES

150 g (5 oz) glacé cherries
1.5 kg (3 lb) mixed dried
    fruit
125 g (4 oz) chopped mixed
    peel
grated rind of 1 orange
60 ml (4 tbsp) Cointreau or
    other orange-flavoured
    liqueur
375 g (13 oz) unsalted
    butter, softened
375 g (13 oz) dark
    muscovado sugar
5 eggs
450 g (1 lb) plain white flour
TO DECORATE
45 ml (3 tbsp) apricot jam
900 g (2 lb) white almond
    paste
ivory food colouring
900 g (2 lb) ready-to-roll
    sugarpaste
1½ metres pearlised beading
pearl lustre dusting powder
selection of fresh flowers,
    such as gerberas, roses, etc

PREPARATION TIME
1½ hours, plus standing
COOKING TIME
3½-4 hours
FREEZING
Suitable: Cake only

420 CALS PER SERVING

1. Quarter the cherries and place in a bowl with the dried fruit, mixed peel and orange rind. Add the liqueur, stir lightly and leave to soak for several hours or overnight.

2. Grease and line a deep 25 cm (10 inch) round cake tin. Preheat the oven to 140°C (275°F) Mark 1. Cream the butter and sugar together in a bowl until soft and fluffy. Beat in the eggs, one at a time, adding a little of the flour to prevent curdling. Sift the remaining flour and fold in. Add the soaked fruits and stir until evenly combined.

3. Turn the cake mixture into the tin and bake for 3½-4 hours or until a skewer inserted in the centre comes out clean. Leave to cool in the tin. Turn out and wrap in a double thickness of foil. Store in a cool place for up to 2 months.

4. To finish the cake, warm the apricot jam and press through a sieve into a bowl. Stir in 15 ml (1 tbsp) hot water. Brush the cake with the glaze and cover with the almond paste (see pages 8-9).

5. Knead a little ivory food colouring into the sugarpaste. Use the icing to cover the cake (see page 9). Roll small balls of icing from the sugarpaste trimmings, the same size as the beads. You will need about 40 of these. Leave to harden overnight.

6. Cut a strip of paper, to fit the circumference and depth of the cake. Fold into 8 equal portions. Make a deep semicircle from two folded points, reaching almost to the base of the strip, and cut out through all thicknesses. Secure around the cake and transfer the curved outline onto the cake, using pin pricks.

7. Secure the beading around the cake over the pin pricks, brushing the area very lightly with water to secure. Cut a single bead and make about 5 impressions below each garland in the icing.

8. Moisten a little dusting powder with water. Roll the balls of icing in the powder, then press into the impressions.

9. Just before the gathering, arrange the flowers on the cake.

TECHNIQUE

Position the beading over the pin-pricked outline, securing with a little water.

PANDA BEAR CAKE

Animals – particularly those associated with cuddly bears – have an affinity with children of all ages! This contented panda sits on a dome-shaped base, made by baking the cake in a pudding basin. Before cutting the cake, the panda, which is made of icing, can be lifted to safety and kept as a momento of the occasion.

MAKES 16 SLICES

175 g (6 oz) self-raising flour
2.5 ml (½ tsp) baking
    powder
30 ml (2 tbsp) cocoa powder
175 g (6 oz) soft margarine
3 eggs
175 g (6 oz) caster sugar
BUTTERCREAM
50 g (2 oz) unsalted butter
    or margarine softened
125 g (4 oz) icing sugar
finely grated rind of ½
    orange
TO DECORATE
60 ml (4 tbsp) apricot glaze
    (see page 76)
1.4 kg (3 lb) sugarpaste
cornflour, for dusting
dark and light green, black,
    brown and yellow food
    colourings
15 ml (1 tbsp) lightly beaten
    egg white
about 125 g (4 oz) icing
    sugar

PREPARATION TIME
1½-2 hours, plus standing time
COOKING TIME
1 hour
FREEZING
Suitable: Cake only

400 CALS PER SLICE

1. Preheat the oven to 160°C (325°F) Mark 3. Grease and base-line a 1.4 litre (2½ pint) pudding basin. In a large bowl, beat together all the ingredients for the cake until smooth. Turn into the basin, level the surface and bake for 1 hour or until firm to touch. Leave to cool in tin.

2. To make the buttercream, beat the ingredients together in a bowl until creamy. Trim the dome of the cake so that it sits flat when inverted. Slice the cake horizontally into three layers, sandwich together with the buttercream and re-assemble on an 18 cm (7 inch) cake board. Brush all over with apricot glaze.

3. Knead dark green food colouring into 700 g (1½ lb) of the sugarpaste. Roll out on a surface dusted with cornflour to a 25 cm (10 inch) round. Lay over the cake, easing the icing around the side to eliminate creases and folds. Trim off excess icing at base. Reserve trimmings.

4. To make the panda, roll 225 g (8 oz) sugarpaste into a ball for the body; stand on a surface and elongate the top of the ball slightly. Roll another 50 g (2 oz) for the head and secure to body, using a lightly dampened paintbrush. Pinch front of head to a point for the snout.

5. Use another 25 g (1 oz) for each leg and 15 g (½ oz) for each arm. Shape and secure. Use a little more sugarpaste to shape ears and secure to the head.

6. Beat the egg white in a bowl, gradually adding the icing sugar until softly peaking. Lightly dampen the panda and brush with the icing to make fur.

7. Colour half the remaining sugarpaste different shades of green, a quarter brown and a quarter yellow. (Keep all icings tightly wrapped.) Roll out each colour separately. Cut out small leaf shapes between 2.5 cm (1 inch) and 5 cm (2 inches) long. Rest over a foil-covered rolling pin and wooden spoon. Leave, with panda, for 24 hours to set.

8. Paint the panda with black colouring. Secure a brown twig and small leaves. Position panda on cake. Place a little icing in a piping bag fitted with a fine writing nozzle and use to pipe claws. Colour remaining icing green and use to secure leaves around panda.

TECHNIQUE

Mould the leg and arm pieces so they sit snugly against the panda's body, securing with a dampened paintbrush.

INDEX

If you would like further information about the **Good Housekeeping Cookery Club**, please write to:
Penny Smith, Ebury Press, Random House, 20 Vauxhall Bridge Road, London SW1V 2SA.
Specialist cake decorating equipment, including food colourings and lustre powders, can be obtained by mail order from SQUIRES KITCHEN, Squires House, 3 Waverley Lane, Farnham, Surrey GL9 8BB: Tel 0252 711749/734309.